# Mrs. Fields®
## I Love Chocolate!
# Cookbook

❖

**100 Easy & Irresistible Recipes**

by Debbi Fields
and the Editors of Time-Life Books

TIME
LIFE
CUSTOM
PUBLISHING

Time-Life Books Inc. Alexandria, Virginia

Time-Life Books
is a division of Time Life Inc.,
a wholly owned subsidiary of
**THE TIME INC. BOOK COMPANY**

**PRESIDENT AND CEO, Time-Life Inc.:**
John Fahey
**PRESIDENT, Time-Life Books:**
John D. Hall

## TIME-LIFE CUSTOM PUBLISHING

**VICE PRESIDENT AND PUBLISHER:**
Terry Newell

*Director of Custom Publishing:*
Frances C. Mangan
*Editorial Director:* Robert A. Doyle
*Director of New Business Development:*
Regina Hall
*Production Manager:* Prudence G. Harris
*Director of Financial Operations:*
J. Brian Birky
*Director of Sales:* Neil Levin
*Financial Analyst:* Trish Palini
*Associate Editor/Research:* Jennifer Pearce
*Associate Manager of Publicity:*
Patricia Loushine

### RETAIL
*Operations Manager:* Dana A. Coleman
*Promotions Manager:* Gary Stoiber
*Sales Manager:* Lorna Milkovich

### CUSTOM PUBLISHING
*Operations Manager:* Phyllis A. Gardner
*Manager, New Business Development:*
Rebecca C. Wheeler
*Special Contributor:* Wendy Blythe

Produced by
**REBUS, INC.**
New York, New York

*Executive Editor:* Kate Slate
*Director of Photography:* Grace Young
*Art Director:* Sara Bowman
*Photographer:* Lisa Koenig

For further information about the recipes in
this book, please write to:
c/o Customer Service
**Mrs. Fields, Inc.**
**333 Main Street**
**Park City, Utah 84060**

**Cover design:** Ron Wilcox
**Cover photograph:** Peter Garfield
**Food stylist:** Lisa Cherkasky

First printing 1994. Printed in U.S.A.
Published simultaneously in Canada.

Time-Life is a trademark of Time Warner
Inc. U.S.A.

Library of Congress Cataloging-in-
Publication Data

Fields, Debbi
    Mrs. Fields I love chocolate! cookbook/by
Debbi Fields and the editors of Time-Life
Books.
        p.        cm.
ISBN 0-8094-7808-0
    1. Cookery (Chocolate)
    I. Time-Life Books.  II. Title.
TX767.C5F54   1994
641.6'374--dc20                    94-2221
                                   CIP

# Contents

❖

# *Introduction*

This book is for people just like me who love great desserts. And that can only begin with chocolate! Before going further, I must admit to my very special feelings about chocolate. You see, I think of chocolate as something more than just a food—I see it as a kind of emotional statement.

Baking for others is a loving act and, in that spirit, chocolate is another way of saying "I love you" or "You're wonderful" or "I care" or "Get well." All desserts send this same message, especially when they're fresh from the oven. But the effect is all that much greater with chocolate because it has a magic all its own. It's truly an expression of how you feel. I guess that's why I love baking for my family so much. I know I won over Randy, my husband of 18 years, with my chocolate chip cookies.

Writing this book has been a learning experience. Before I set about making these recipes, there were categories of desserts that I tended to avoid because I assumed they were too complex or too fussy. In developing these recipes, however, I learned that even the supposedly troublesome soufflés, candies, and pies could be made successfully—even easily—as

long as they were clearly explained. You don't have to graduate from pastry school to be able to make my recipes. This is a book for everybody. (That's proven by the assessment of my five children, who were involved in helping me create and—certainly—eat these recipes.)

In our Showstoppers section, the recipes require a few more preparation steps and take a little bit more fuss, but wait until you taste those recipes. I know you'll say "Wow!" Especially when you taste the Floating Heaven or the Triple Chocolate Suicide or the Layered Chocolate Peanut Butter Cheesecake. They are really incredible.

When I create recipes, I'm always interested in both taste and texture. For example, when we made the Chocolate Malibu, we were experimenting with the way the different flavors and textures worked together. The Chocolate Angel Pie was also wonderful with its creamy, luscious, smooth filling, blended with a light and crumbly meringue crust.

The most important thing to me was to make the desserts for this book taste great! And the measurement of that was whether or not I had to stop myself from eating it all. When that happened, I knew we were on to something good. The second screening test was serving the desserts to my family and friends and watching their eyes light up when they took the first bite.

The most useful advice when it comes to making these recipes is to use the best ingredients you can find. If possible, use butter—it does taste better in baked goods. Toast nuts before baking with them; it enhances the nutty flavor. And always use real, or "pure," vanilla. Pay particular attention to the chocolate you buy, especially when it comes to white chocolate. Cocoa butter content is the mark of a superior white chocolate. With milk chocolate and dark chocolate you want to buy brands that you like, of course, but the key is to be able to really taste the quality. If you enjoy a particular type of chocolate candy bar, you can bet that same chocolate will be great in your cookies.

With dark chocolate, pay attention to whether a recipe calls for sweet, semisweet (or bittersweet), or unsweetened chocolate. You don't want to inadvertently substitute one of these ingredients for another.

When you store chocolate, it will have a tendency to absorb flavors around it, so keep your supply tightly wrapped and keep it away from the spices, garlic, and onions in your pantry. Dark chocolate ages and will actually develop a better taste over time. Milk chocolate doesn't have a long shelf life, so use it up by making these fun, wonderful recipes.

Whenever possible, serve your desserts while they are still very fresh—first, because they are irresistible that way, but, more importantly, because they are gifts from the heart. They are all the more special when presented fresh from the oven surrounded by that irresistible aroma. You can taste the difference and it makes a difference.

When you can't serve the desserts immediately, however, it's reassuring to know that many of the treats in this book keep quite nicely in the freezer. Brownies and cookies will be good for six months, as long as you freeze them sealed in plastic bags. We also have a recipe called

Chocolate Chip Dough to Go, which will allow you to serve fresh baked cookies at a few minutes notice. This one has been a real time-saver for me, and my kids love to bake them up.

The candies are best stored in the refrigerator to keep them from melting. And for recipes such as Debbi's Deadly Chocolate Muffins, it's best to keep them covered but not sealed. They're going to get mushy rather quickly if you store them in sealed plastic containers. Cookies, on the other hand, will stay softer and chewier if you keep them in airtight containers.

As for equipment, you don't need to go out and buy anything. A double boiler helps, but purely as insurance against burning your expensive chocolate. For most of the recipes in this book, you'll be melting chocolate and butter. You can do this without a double boiler, but you'll have to be very attentive and stir constantly. You can also improvise a double boiler with two saucepans nested together.

Chocolate can also be melted in the microwave. Cook on low heat and for intervals of no longer than 15 seconds. Stir between each of these intervals because the chocolate tends to hold its form in the microwave, and it may lull you into burning it.

I hope these recipes give you as much joy as they have already given me and my family.

# Cookies & Bars

# Double-Chocolate Peanut Butter Cookies

6 ounces semisweet chocolate, coarsely
chopped
2 cups all-purpose flour
½ teaspoon baking soda
¼ teaspoon salt
¾ cup (packed) dark brown sugar
¾ cup granulated sugar
2 sticks (1 cup) unsalted butter
1 cup creamy peanut butter
2 large eggs
2 teaspoons vanilla extract
12 ounces milk chocolate chips
(about 2 cups)
24 to 30 whole shelled peanuts

YIELD: *About 2 dozen*

Preheat the oven to 300°. In a double boiler, melt the semisweet chocolate over hot, not simmering, water. Set aside to cool to room temperature.

In a small bowl, whisk together the flour, baking soda, and salt.

In a medium bowl, whisk together the brown and granulated sugars, then add the butter and beat until well combined. Add the peanut butter and beat until smooth. Add the eggs and vanilla, and beat until just combined. Add the flour mixture and the milk chocolate chips, and beat until no streaks of flour are visible.

Pour in the melted chocolate and mix partially with a wooden spoon until marbled. Drop the dough in 3-tablespoon mounds 2 inches apart on an ungreased baking sheet. Top with one whole peanut. Bake for 23 minutes, or until just set but still soft. Cool on the cookie sheet for 30 seconds, then transfer to a wire rack to cool completely.

*Near right, beat the peanut butter into the butter-sugar mixture. Far right, before baking, press a whole peanut into the center of each mound of cookie dough.*

# White Chocolate Cookies with Chocolate Chunks

Preheat the oven to 300°. Cut 4 tablespoons of the butter into ¼-inch cubes.

In a small bowl, whisk together the flour, baking soda, and salt.

In a double boiler, melt the white chocolate with the butter, stirring until melted and smooth, about 10 minutes. Set aside to cool slightly.

In a large bowl with an electric mixer, cream the remaining 1½ sticks of butter with the granulated and brown sugars. Beat in the eggs one at a time, beating well after each addition. Beat in the white chocolate mixture and the vanilla. On low speed, gradually beat in the flour mixture until just combined. Stir in the semisweet chocolate chunks.

Drop the dough by rounded tablespoon 2 inches apart onto an ungreased cookie sheet. Bake for about 20 minutes, or until the edges of the cookies begin to brown lightly (the cookies will still be soft in the center). Cool on the cookie sheet for 1 minute, then transfer to a wire rack to cool completely.

*2 sticks (1 cup) unsalted butter, softened*
*2½ cups all-purpose flour*
*1 teaspoon baking soda*
*¼ teaspoon salt*
*3 ounces white chocolate, finely chopped*
*½ cup granulated sugar*
*½ cup (packed) light brown sugar*
*2 large eggs, at room temperature*
*2 teaspoons vanilla extract*
*8 ounces semisweet chocolate, cut into chunks*

YIELD: *About 3 dozen*

# Best White Chocolate Butterscotch Cookies

2½ cups all-purpose flour
1 teaspoon baking soda
¼ teaspoon salt
2 sticks (1 cup) unsalted butter,
softened
1½ cups (packed) dark brown sugar
2 large eggs
1 tablespoon light molasses
2 teaspoons vanilla extract
1 teaspoon Scotch whiskey
1 cup chopped pecans, toasted
¾ cup butterscotch chips
¾ cup white chocolate chips

YIELD: *About 3 dozen*

Preheat the oven to 300°.

In a medium bowl, whisk together the flour, baking soda, and salt.

In a large bowl with an electric mixer, cream the butter and sugar. Add the eggs, molasses, vanilla, and whiskey, then blend well. Add the flour mixture and mix to blend. Stir in the pecans, butterscotch chips, and white chocolate chips. Do not overmix.

Drop the cookie dough by rounded tablespoon 2 inches apart onto an ungreased cookie sheet. Bake for 18 to 20 minutes, or until set. Transfer to wire racks to cool.

# Double-Dipped Chocolate Shortbread Cookies

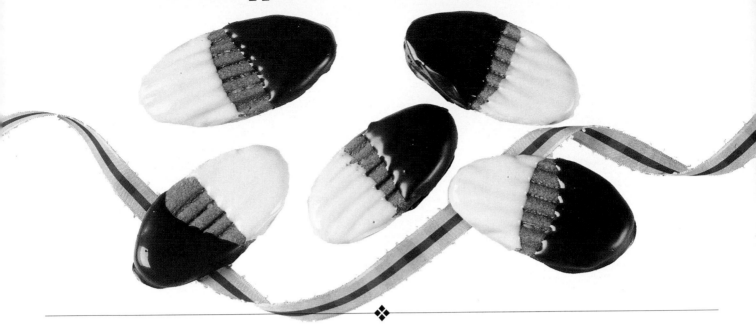

**MAKE THE COOKIES:** In a double boiler, melt the semisweet chocolate over hot, not simmering, water. Set aside to cool to lukewarm.

In a large bowl with an electric mixer, cream the butter. Beat in the melted chocolate. Then beat in the vanilla, flour, sugar, cocoa, and salt. Wrap and chill the dough for 30 minutes, or until firm enough to roll into balls.

Preheat the oven to 350°. Roll the dough into 1-inch balls, then roll each ball into a thick log. Place on an ungreased cookie sheet and press the dough to a ¼-inch thickness with the tines of a fork, keeping the cookies oval in shape.

Bake the cookies for 8 to 10 minutes, or until just set; do not overbake. Transfer to wire racks to cool completely.

**DIP THE COOKIES:** In a small bowl set over a saucepan of hot water, melt the white chocolate with ¼ cup of the cream; stir until smooth. Keep the mixture over the hot water so it will be liquid for dipping. In another small bowl set over a saucepan of hot water, melt the semisweet chocolate with the remaining ¼ cup cream; stir until smooth. Keep warm.

Dip one end of a cookie in the white chocolate and the other end in the dark chocolate and return to the cooling racks so the chocolate can set. Repeat with the remaining cookies.

### COOKIES

*3 ounces semisweet chocolate, finely chopped*
*1½ sticks (¾ cup) unsalted butter, softened*
*1 teaspoon vanilla extract*
*1½ cups all-purpose flour*
*½ cup confectioners' sugar*
*2 teaspoons unsweetened cocoa powder*
*⅛ teaspoon salt*

### FOR DIPPING

*4 ounces white chocolate, finely chopped*
*½ cup heavy cream*
*3 ounces semisweet chocolate, finely chopped*

YIELD: *About 2½ dozen*

2 cups all-purpose flour
1 cup old-fashioned rolled oats
½ teaspoon baking soda
¼ teaspoon salt
2 sticks (1 cup) unsalted butter
1⅓ cups (packed) dark brown sugar
2 large eggs
2 teaspoons vanilla extract
12 ounces semisweet chocolate, cut into large chunks

YIELD: *15 large cookies*

Preheat the oven to 300°. In a medium bowl, whisk together the flour, oats, baking soda, and salt.

In a large bowl with an electric mixer, cream the butter. Beat in the sugar and continue to beat until well combined. Beat in the eggs, one at a time, then add the vanilla. On low speed, blend in the flour mixture, stirring in the last bit with a wooden spoon. Stir in the chocolate chunks.

Divide the dough into 15 equal portions. Place the portions of dough 3 inches apart on an ungreased cookie sheet and pat into disks ½ inch thick.

Bake for 20 to 22 minutes, or until lightly browned on the underside. Cool on the cookie sheet for 1 minute, then carefully transfer to a wire rack to cool completely.

*Before baking, press each mound of cookie dough to a ½-inch thickness.*

# *Brownie Nuggets*

Preheat the oven to 350°. Line 24 mini-muffin cups with paper liners.

MAKE THE BROWNIES: In a double boiler, melt the chocolate chips with the butter, stirring until smooth. Set aside to cool to room temperature.

In a small bowl, whisk together the flour and salt.

In a medium bowl, beat the eggs and sugar until thick and pale. Stir in the vanilla and the cooled chocolate mixture until well blended. Stir in the flour mixture until just combined.

Dividing evenly, spoon the batter into the muffin cups. Bake for 12 to 15 minutes, or until the edges are set but the centers are still moist and fudgy. Cool the brownies in the pan on a rack for 15 minutes. Remove from the pan to cool completely.

PREPARE THE GANACHE: Place the white chocolate in a medium bowl. In a small saucepan, bring the cream to a simmer. Pour the hot cream over the chocolate. Let stand, covered, for 5 minutes, then stir until smooth. Stir in the butter until incorporated and smooth. Refrigerate the ganache until it is thickened but still pourable.

DIP THE BROWNIE NUGGETS: Dip the tops of the brownies in the ganache. Refrigerate to set the ganache. Dip the brownies in the ganache again for a second coat. Chill to set the ganache.

### BROWNIES
*6 ounces semisweet chocolate chips (about 1 cup)*
*1 stick (½ cup) unsalted butter*
*½ cup plus 2 tablespoons all-purpose flour*
*¼ teaspoon salt*
*2 large eggs*
*¾ cup (packed) light brown sugar*
*1 teaspoon vanilla extract*

### WHITE CHOCOLATE GANACHE
*9 ounces white chocolate, finely chopped*
*½ cup heavy cream*
*1 tablespoon unsalted butter*

YIELD: *2 dozen*

# Chocolate Coconut Crunch Cookies

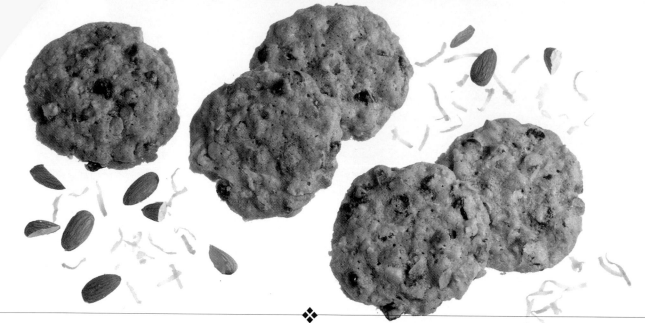

2 cups all-purpose flour
1 teaspoon baking soda
¼ teaspoon salt
2 sticks (1 cup) unsalted butter, softened
¾ cup (packed) light brown sugar
¾ cup granulated sugar
2 large eggs, lightly beaten
2 teaspoons vanilla extract
1 teaspoon almond extract
2 cups shredded coconut
12 ounces semisweet chocolate chips (about 2 cups)
1½ cups lightly salted, dry-roasted almonds, finely chopped

YIELD: *About 4 dozen*

Preheat the oven to 300°.

In a small bowl, whisk together the flour, baking soda, and salt.

In a medium bowl with an electric mixer, cream the butter and sugars. Beat in the eggs, vanilla, and almond extract. Mix on low speed until blended. Add the flour mixture and mix just until blended; do not overmix. Add the coconut, chocolate chips, and almonds and stir until just incorporated.

Drop the dough by rounded tablespoon 2 inches apart onto an ungreased cookie sheet. Bake for 18 to 20 minutes, or until set. Transfer to wire racks to cool.

# Coconut Mud Bars

❖

Preheat the oven to 350°. Lightly butter a 9-by-13-inch baking pan.

MAKE THE BOTTOM LAYER: In a medium bowl, whisk together the flour, baking powder, salt, and brown sugar. With a pastry blender, cut the butter into the dry ingredients until the mixture resembles coarse meal. Press the mixture into the bottom of the prepared pan. Bake for 10 minutes, or until the crust is just set. Place the pan on a rack to cool, but leave the oven on.

MEANWHILE, MAKE THE GANACHE: Place the chocolate in a medium bowl. In a small saucepan, bring the cream to a simmer. Pour the hot cream over the chocolate; let stand for 5 minutes, then stir until smooth. Pour the ganache over the crust and refrigerate for about 15 minutes to set the ganache.

PREPARE THE TOPPING: In a medium bowl, cream the butter. Add the granulated sugar, vanilla, and coconut extract (optional) and beat until blended. Beat in the eggs. Stir in the coconut and pecans.

Drop the coconut-pecan topping evenly over the ganache and spread gently. Bake for 25 to 30 minutes, or until the top is golden brown. Set the pan on a wire rack to cool. Cut into bars.

### BOTTOM LAYER
*1⅓ cups all-purpose flour*
*½ teaspoon baking powder*
*Pinch of salt*
*½ cup (packed) dark brown sugar*
*1 stick (½ cup) unsalted butter, slightly softened and cut into small pieces*

### GANACHE
*10 ounces semisweet chocolate, finely chopped*
*¾ cup heavy cream*

### TOPPING
*4 tablespoons (¼ cup) unsalted butter, softened*
*½ cup granulated sugar*
*2 teaspoons vanilla extract*
*¼ teaspoon coconut extract (optional)*
*2 large eggs*
*1½ cups shredded coconut*
*1½ cups chopped pecans*

### YIELD: *24 bars*

*Melt the chocolate for the ganache by pouring hot cream over finely chopped chocolate. Let stand for about 5 minutes, then stir until melted and smooth.*

# Golden White-Chunk Nutty Bars

2 cups all-purpose flour
½ teaspoon baking soda
¼ teaspoon salt
1½ sticks (¾ cup) unsalted butter,
cut into tablespoons
1 cup (packed) dark brown sugar
2 eggs
½ cup shredded coconut
2 teaspoons vanilla extract
10 ounces white chocolate, coarsely
chopped
1 cup coarsely chopped pecans

YIELD: *16 bars*

Preheat the oven to 300°. Butter a 9-by-13-inch baking pan.

In a medium bowl, whisk together the flour, baking soda, and salt.

In another medium bowl with an electric mixer, cream the butter and sugar. Beat in the eggs, coconut, and vanilla, then blend slowly until smooth. Add the flour mixture, chopped chocolate, and pecans.

Scrape the dough into the prepared baking pan and level and smooth the surface. Bake for 40 to 45 minutes, or until the center is set and the top is golden.

Place the pan on a wire rack to cool to room temperature before cutting into 16 bars.

# Chocolate Cashew Crunch

Preheat the oven to 350°. Butter and flour a cookie sheet.

In a small saucepan, melt the butter over medium heat. Add the brown sugar and corn syrup, then bring to a boil over medium heat, stirring constantly until the sugar dissolves, 3 to 5 minutes. Remove from the heat.

Stir in the cashews, flour, and vanilla. Drop the batter into ½-teaspoon mounds 2 inches apart on the prepared cookie sheet. Using a small spatula, spread each mound into a circle.

Bake for 8 to 10 minutes, or until browned, rotating the pan back to front after 4 minutes. Cool on the cookie sheet for about 30 seconds, then transfer to wire racks to cool completely.

In a small bowl set over a small saucepan, melt the chocolate over hot, not simmering, water. Dip the cookies halfway into the chocolate and return to the racks to set.

*4 tablespoons (¼ cup) unsalted butter*
*⅓ cup (packed) light brown sugar*
*¼ cup light corn syrup*
*½ cup finely chopped salted cashews*
*⅓ cup all-purpose flour*
*1½ teaspoons vanilla extract*
*6 ounces milk chocolate chips (about 1 cup)*

YIELD: *About 3 dozen*

# Chippity Chippers

2¾ cups cake flour
1 teaspoon baking soda
½ teaspoon salt
2 sticks (1 cup) unsalted butter,
softened
½ cup (packed) light brown sugar
½ cup granulated sugar
1 tablespoon honey
2 large eggs
2 teaspoons vanilla extract
6 ounces semisweet chocolate chips
(about 1 cup)
6 ounces milk chocolate chips
(about 1 cup)
6 ounces white chocolate chips
(about 1 cup)
3 ounces peanut butter chips
(about ½ cup)

YIELD: *About 3 dozen*

Preheat the oven to 325°.

In a medium bowl, whisk together the flour, baking soda, and salt.

In a medium bowl, cream the butter, sugars, and honey. Add the eggs one at a time, beating well after each addition. Beat in the vanilla. Stir in the flour mixture and all of the chips. Stir just until blended; do not overmix.

Drop the dough by rounded tablespoon 2 inches apart on an ungreased cookie sheet. Bake for 18 to 20 minutes. Transfer to wire racks to cool.

# Cherry Cream Bars

Preheat the oven to 300°. Butter a 7-by-11-inch baking pan.

MAKE THE BROWNIE LAYER: In a large bowl, whisk together the flour, granulated sugar, brown sugar, and salt.

In a double boiler, melt the unsweetened chocolate and butter together over low heat, stirring until smooth.

In a small bowl, lightly beat the eggs with the milk and vanilla.

Add the chocolate mixture and beaten eggs to the dry ingredients and stir to blend. Stir in the walnuts, cherries, and chocolate chips.

Pour the batter into the prepared pan and bake for 1 hour and 10 minutes, or until a cake tester inserted in the center comes out with a few crumbs clinging to it. Cool the brownies in the pan on a rack.

MEANWHILE, MAKE THE CHOCOLATE-CHERRY GLAZE: Place the semisweet chocolate in a medium bowl.

In a small saucepan, bring the reserved cherry syrup to a boil. Simmer until reduced by half. Add the cream and bring to a boil. Remove from the heat and stir in the kirsch and granulated sugar.

Pour the hot cream mixture over the chocolate. Let stand, covered, for 5 minutes, then stir until smooth. Set aside to cool to room temperature, then pour the glaze over the cooled brownies.

MAKE THE CHERRY CREAM: In a medium bowl, beat the cream with the confectioners' sugar and kirsch until stiff peaks form. Fold in the drained chopped cherries.

Cut into 12 bars and serve with a spoonful of cherry cream on top.

### BROWNIE LAYER
*1 cup all-purpose flour*
*1 cup granulated sugar*
*¾ cup (packed) dark brown sugar*
*½ teaspoon salt*
*4 ounces unsweetened chocolate*
*1½ sticks (¾ cup) unsalted butter*
*4 large eggs*
*¼ cup milk*
*2½ teaspoons vanilla extract*
*1 cup coarsely chopped walnuts*
*1 cup drained canned Bing cherries*
*(½ cup of the syrup reserved)*
*1 cup semisweet chocolate chips*

### CHOCOLATE-CHERRY GLAZE
*3 ounces semisweet chocolate, chopped*
*½ cup syrup reserved from cherries*
*¼ cup heavy cream*
*2 teaspoons kirsch (cherry brandy)*
*2 teaspoons granulated sugar*

### CHERRY CREAM
*1 cup heavy cream*
*3 tablespoons confectioners' sugar*
*1 tablespoon kirsch (cherry brandy)*
*½ cup chopped drained canned Bing cherries*

YIELD: *12 bars*

4 tablespoons (¼ cup) unsalted
butter
¼ cup (packed) light brown sugar
¼ cup light corn syrup
⅓ cup all-purpose flour
½ cup finely chopped unsalted
peanuts
1 teaspoon vanilla extract
4 ounces semisweet chocolate, finely
chopped

YIELD: *About 16 sandwich cookies*

Preheat the oven to 350°. Butter and flour a cookie sheet.

In a small saucepan, melt the butter over medium heat. Add the brown sugar and corn syrup and bring to a boil over medium heat, stirring constantly until the sugar dissolves, 3 to 5 minutes. Remove the pan from the heat and stir in the flour, peanuts, and vanilla.

Quickly drop the batter in ½-teaspoon mounds 2 inches apart on the prepared cookie sheet. Using a small spatula, spread each mound into an even circle.

Bake for 9 to 10 minutes, or until browned; rotate the pan back to front halfway through the baking time. Cool on the cookie sheet for 1 to 2 minutes, then transfer to a wire rack to cool completely.

In a double boiler, melt the chocolate over hot, not simmering, water. Spread a thin layer of chocolate over the bottom (flat side) of one cookie. Cover with another cookie and gently press together. Repeat with the remaining cookies. Refrigerate the cookies to set the chocolate.

Lightly butter a 7-by-11-inch or an 8-inch square baking pan.

In a large saucepan, melt the butter over low heat. Add the marshmallows and stir until blended. Remove from the heat and stir in the vanilla.

Stir in the cereal and mix with a wooden spoon until thoroughly blended. Scrape the mixture into the prepared pan. With lightly buttered hands or a lightly buttered spatula, press gently on the mixture to level. Place in the freezer for 10 minutes.

In a small saucepan, warm the butterscotch caramel fudge topping to lukewarm (do not let it get hot). Remove from the heat and set aside to cool slightly.

Pour the warm butterscotch topping over the cereal layer, spreading evenly. Place in the freezer for 10 minutes.

In a double boiler, melt the chocolate over hot, not simmering, water. Set aside to cool slightly. Spread the chocolate on top of the caramel mixture. Chill to set the chocolate. Cut into squares and serve.

*4 tablespoons (¼ cup) unsalted butter*
*4 cups miniature marshmallows*
*2 teaspoons vanilla extract*
*4 cups crisp rice cereal*
*¾ cup butterscotch caramel fudge topping*
*12 ounces milk chocolate, coarsely chopped*

YIELD: *16 squares*

# Chocolate Chip Cookies with Toasted Pecans

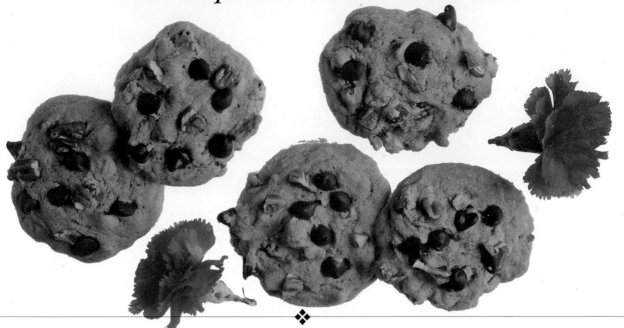

2½ cups all-purpose flour
1 teaspoon baking soda
¼ teaspoon salt
2 sticks (1 cup) unsalted butter,
softened
1 cup (packed) dark brown sugar
½ cup granulated sugar
2 large eggs
2 teaspoons vanilla extract
1 cup chopped pecans, toasted
12 ounces semisweet chocolate chips
(about 2 cups)

YIELD: *About 3 dozen*

Preheat the oven to 300°.

In a medium bowl, whisk together the flour, baking soda, and salt.

In a large bowl with an electric mixer, cream the butter and sugars. Beat in the eggs and vanilla until just combined.

Add the flour mixture, toasted pecans, and chocolate chips, then beat on low speed until just blended.

Drop the dough by rounded tablespoon 2 inches apart on an ungreased cookie sheet. Bake for 15 to 20 minutes, or until golden. Transfer to wire racks to cool.

Preheat the oven to 325°. Butter a 7-by-11-inch baking pan.

**PREPARE THE BROWNIE LAYER:** In a double boiler, melt the unsweetened chocolate and butter together, stirring until smooth. Set aside to cool slightly.

In a small bowl, whisk together the flour and salt.

In a medium bowl, beat the eggs and brown sugar together. Beat in the chocolate mixture and the vanilla. Stir in the flour mixture. Then stir in the pecans and mini chocolate chips.

Spread the batter in the prepared pan and bake for 22 to 25 minutes, or until a cake tester inserted in the center comes out clean. Cool in the pan on a rack.

**MAKE THE VANILLA CREAM:** In a medium bowl, cream the butter and cream cheese until light and fluffy. Gradually beat in the vanilla and confectioners' sugar. Spread the vanilla cream over the cooled brownies. Refrigerate until set.

**PREPARE THE DRIZZLE:** In a double boiler, melt the chocolate chips and cream over hot, not simmering, water. Stir until smooth, then set aside to cool slightly. Dip a fork into the melted chocolate mixture and drizzle in a random pattern over the vanilla cream layer.

Chill until ready to serve.

### BROWNIE LAYER
*4 ounces unsweetened chocolate*
*1 stick (½ cup) salted butter*
*¾ cup all-purpose flour*
*¼ teaspoon salt*
*2 large eggs*
*1 cup (packed) light brown sugar*
*2 teaspoons vanilla extract*
*½ cup chopped pecans*
*½ cup mini semisweet chocolate chips*

### VANILLA CREAM
*1 stick (½ cup) salted butter*
*4 ounces cream cheese, softened*
*1 teaspoon vanilla extract*
*1¼ cups confectioners' sugar*

### CHOCOLATE DRIZZLE
*2 ounces semisweet chocolate chips*
*2 tablespoons heavy cream*

**YIELD:** *16 bars*

# Fudge Cookies with White Chocolate

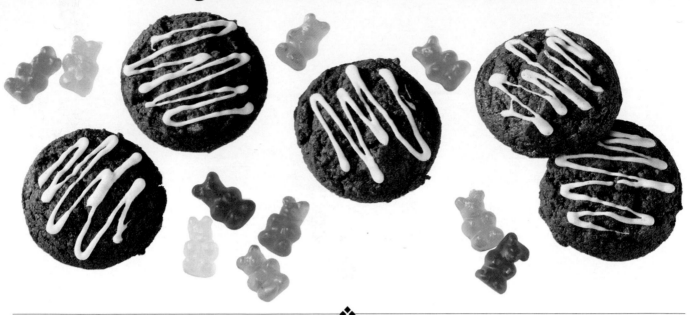

12 ounces semisweet chocolate, finely
chopped
2 cups all-purpose flour
¾ cup unsweetened cocoa powder
1 teaspoon baking soda
¼ teaspoon salt
2 sticks (1 cup) unsalted butter,
softened
1½ cups (packed) dark brown sugar
3 large eggs, at room temperature
2 teaspoons vanilla extract
4 ounces white chocolate, coarsely
chopped
1 teaspoon vegetable oil

YIELD: *About 3 dozen*

Preheat the oven to 300°.

In a double boiler, melt the semisweet chocolate over hot, not simmering, water. Set aside to cool slightly.

In a medium bowl, whisk together the flour, cocoa, baking soda, and salt.

In a large bowl with an electric mixer, cream the butter and sugar. Beat in the eggs and vanilla until just combined. Blend in the cooled semisweet chocolate. Blend in the flour mixture until just combined.

Drop the dough by rounded tablespoon 2 inches apart on an ungreased cookie sheet. Bake for 18 to 22 minutes, or until set. Cool on the cookie sheet for 1 minute, then transfer to a wire rack to cool completely.

In a double boiler, melt the white chocolate with the oil over hot, not simmering, water. Set aside to cool slightly.

Dip a fork into the melted white chocolate and drizzle over the cookies.

# Mother Lode Brownies

Preheat the oven to 325°. Butter and flour a 9-by-9-inch baking pan.

**MAKE THE BROWNIE LAYER:** In a small bowl, whisk together the flour and baking soda.

In a double boiler, melt the unsweetened chocolate and the semisweet chocolate with the butter. Stir until smooth and set aside to cool slightly.

In a large bowl with an electric mixer, beat the brown sugar and eggs until lightened and pale in color. Beat in the cooled chocolate mixture and the vanilla. Gradually beat in the flour mixture.

Pour the batter into the prepared pan. Bake for 40 to 50 minutes, or until the center is set but still moist and a bit fudgy. Cool in the pan on a wire rack.

**PREPARE THE CARAMEL LAYER:** In a small heavy saucepan, dissolve the sugar in the water over low heat, stirring constantly. Bring to a boil over medium-high heat, then let boil without stirring until the syrup turns a deep amber. While the syrup is boiling, brush down the sides of the pan from time to time with a wet pastry brush to prevent crystals from forming. Remove the pan from the heat, then stir in the hot cream (be careful, it will bubble rapidly). Continue stirring, over low heat if necessary, until all of the caramel is dissolved into the cream. Stir in the butter until smooth. Set the caramel aside until it has cooled slightly but is still spreadable.

**TO ASSEMBLE:** Preheat the oven to 325°. Spread the caramel over the cooled brownie. Sprinkle the toppings—macadamia nuts, semisweet chips, and milk chocolate chips—over the caramel layer and place the brownies in the oven for 5 minutes to set the topping (do not let the chips melt completely).

Set on a wire rack to cool, then cut into squares.

**BROWNIE LAYER**
*¾ cup all-purpose flour*
*¼ teaspoon baking soda*
*3 ounces unsweetened chocolate*
*3 ounces semisweet chocolate*
*1½ sticks (¾ cup) unsalted butter*
*1½ cups (packed) light brown sugar*
*3 large eggs*
*2 teaspoons vanilla extract*

**CARAMEL LAYER**
*¾ cup granulated sugar*
*3 tablespoons water*
*¼ cup heavy cream, scalded*
*2 tablespoons unsalted butter*

**TOPPINGS**
*1 cup coarsely chopped macadamia nuts*
*9 ounces semisweet chocolate chips (about 1½ cups)*
*6 ounces milk chocolate chips (about 1 cup)*

**YIELD:** *15 brownies*

# Pumpkin Harvest Cookies

2¼ cups all-purpose flour
1 teaspoon pumpkin pie spice
½ teaspoon baking soda
2 sticks (1 cup) unsalted butter
1½ cups (packed) dark brown sugar
1 cup solid-pack unsweetened
pumpkin purée
2 large eggs
1 tablespoon vanilla extract
10 ounces white chocolate, coarsely
chopped
1 cup pecan halves and pieces,
toasted

YIELD: *About 3 dozen*

Preheat the oven to 300°.

In a small bowl, whisk together the flour, pumpkin pie spice, and baking soda.

In a medium bowl with an electric mixer, cream the butter and sugar. Beat in the pumpkin purée. Beat in the eggs and vanilla. Beat in the flour mixture until just combined. Stir in the white chocolate and pecans.

Drop the dough by rounded tablespoon 2 inches apart on an ungreased cookie sheet. Bake for 20 to 22 minutes, or until just set. Transfer to a wire rack to cool.

# Chocolate Chip Dough to Go

In a medium bowl, whisk together the flour, oats, baking powder, and salt. In another medium bowl with an electric mixer, cream the butter and sugars. Beat in the eggs and vanilla. Gently beat in the flour mixture; then stir in the pecans and chocolate chips.

Turn half of the dough out onto a sheet of wax paper. Shape into a log 2 inches in diameter. Roll up the log of dough in the wax paper and twist the ends closed. Repeat with the remaining dough. Chill until firm. The cookie dough can be refrigerated for 1 week or frozen for 6 months stored in an airtight plastic bag.

To bake the cookies, preheat the oven to 300°. If using frozen dough, let it soften slightly at room temperature, then cut the dough log into ½-inch-thick slices. Place the slices on a cookie sheet 2 inches apart. Bake for 22 to 24 minutes, or until set.

*2 cups all-purpose flour*
*1 cup quick oats*
*½ teaspoon baking powder*
*¼ teaspoon salt*
*2 sticks (1 cup) unsalted butter, softened*
*¾ cup (packed) light brown sugar*
*¾ cup granulated sugar*
*2 large eggs*
*2 teaspoons vanilla extract*
*1 cup coarsely chopped pecans*
*12 ounces semisweet chocolate chips (about 2 cups)*

YIELD: *About 4 dozen*

*Cut the chilled dough into ½-inch slices and place 2 inches apart on an ungreased cookie sheet.*

27

❖

*2¼ cups all-purpose flour*
*1 teaspoon baking soda*
*1½ sticks (¾ cup) unsalted butter,*
*softened*
*1 cup (packed) dark brown sugar*
*2 large eggs*
*2 teaspoons vanilla extract*
*1⅓ cups shredded coconut*
*12 ounces white chocolate, cut into*
*chunks*
*1 cup coarsely chopped macadamia*
*nuts*

Yield: *About 3 dozen*

Preheat the oven to 300°.

In a small bowl, whisk together the flour and baking soda.

In a medium bowl with an electric mixer, cream the butter and sugar. Beat in the eggs and vanilla. Beat in the flour mixture; do not overmix. Stir in the coconut, white chocolate chunks, and macadamia nuts.

Drop the dough by rounded tablespoon 2 inches apart on an ungreased cookie sheet. Bake for 18 to 20 minutes. Transfer to a wire rack to cool.

# Reduced-Fat Chocolate Brownies

Preheat the oven to 325°. Spray an 8-inch square baking pan with non-stick cooking spray.

In a small heavy saucepan, bring the water to a boil. Add the prunes, cover, reduce the heat, and simmer for 5 minutes. Remove from the heat and set aside to steep for 5 minutes. Uncover and let cool to room temperature. Drain the liquid and purée the prunes.

In a small bowl, whisk together the flour, cocoa, baking powder, and salt.

In a medium bowl with an electric mixer, cream the butter and sugar. Beat in the prune purée, applesauce, and vanilla. Beat in the egg whites. Beat in the flour mixture.

Spread the batter in the prepared pan and smooth the top. Sprinkle with the chocolate chips, if desired. Bake for 35 to 40 minutes, or until the center springs back when lightly pressed; do not overbake.

Cool in the pan on a rack, then cut into 16 squares.

½ cup water
3 ounces pitted prunes (about 9 prunes)
¾ cup plus 1 tablespoon all-purpose flour
½ cup unsweetened cocoa powder
½ teaspoon baking powder
¼ teaspoon salt
4 tablespoons (¼ cup) unsalted butter
1 cup (packed) light brown sugar
½ cup unsweetened applesauce
2 teaspoons vanilla extract
4 egg whites
¼ cup mini semisweet chocolate chips (optional)

YIELD: *16 brownies*

# Low-Fat Chocolate Cookies

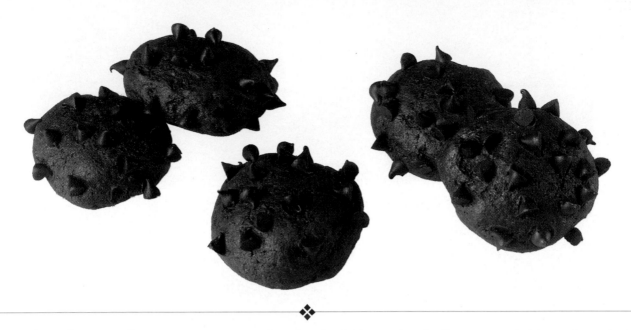

2⅔ cups all-purpose flour
½ cup unsweetened cocoa powder
1 teaspoon baking soda
½ teaspoon salt
¾ cup (packed) dark brown sugar
¾ cup granulated sugar
⅓ cup canola oil
½ cup unsweetened applesauce
3 egg whites
2 teaspoons vanilla extract
½ cup mini semisweet chocolate chips

YIELD: *About 5½ dozen*

In a medium bowl, whisk together the flour, cocoa, baking soda, and salt.

In another medium bowl, with an electric mixer, blend the brown and granulated sugars. Slowly beat in the oil. Beat in the applesauce, egg whites, and vanilla, and blend on low speed until smooth.

Add the flour mixture and blend on low speed until the dough is just combined. Refrigerate the dough until firm, about 1 hour.

Preheat the oven to 300°.

Roll the dough into small (1-inch) balls, place on a cookie sheet and flatten slightly. Sprinkle with the mini chocolate chips, then bake for 17 to 19 minutes (do not overbake; when the cookies cool they will get hard). Transfer the cookies to a wire rack to cool.

# *Cakes*

# Swiss Chocolate Cheesecake

### CRUST
*1½ cups vanilla wafer crumbs*
*4 tablespoons unsalted butter, melted*
*½ cup finely ground toasted almonds*

### FILLING
*16 ounces milk chocolate, finely chopped*
*1½ pounds cream cheese, softened*
*1 cup sugar*
*¼ teaspoon salt*
*4 large eggs*
*½ cup light cream or half-and-half*
*2 teaspoons vanilla extract*

### CHOCOLATE GLAZE
*2 ounces semisweet chocolate, coarsely chopped*
*3 tablespoons unsalted butter*
*¼ cup water*
*2 tablespoons unsweetened cocoa powder*
*2 tablespoons light corn syrup*
*⅓ cup sugar*
*1 teaspoon vanilla extract*

*Milk chocolate curls, for garnish*

YIELD: *One 9-inch cake*

Preheat the oven to 300°.

MAKE THE CRUST: In a medium bowl, combine the cookie crumbs, butter, and almonds until well blended. Press the moistened crumbs into the bottom and 1½ inches up the sides of a 9-inch springform pan.

PREPARE THE FILLING: In a double boiler, melt the milk chocolate over hot, not simmering, water. Set aside to cool slightly.

In a large bowl with an electric mixer, beat the cream cheese until creamy. Add the sugar and salt and beat until blended. Beat in the eggs one at a time, beating well after each addition. Stir in the melted chocolate, cream, and vanilla until well blended.

Pour the batter into the prepared crust and bake for 1 hour. Turn off the heat but leave the cheesecake in the oven for 1 hour. Remove from the oven and set on a wire rack to cool to room temperature.

MEANWHILE, MAKE THE CHOCOLATE GLAZE: In a small saucepan, combine the semisweet chocolate, butter, water, and cocoa. Stir over low heat until melted and smooth. Add the corn syrup and sugar, then stir until the sugar dissolves. Increase the heat and bring the sauce to a low boil, then cook until the sauce thickens, 12 to 15 minutes. Remove from the heat, stir in the vanilla, and set aside to cool to room temperature.

Pour the cooled glaze over the room-temperature cheesecake. Chill until firm, 6 to 8 hours. Sprinkle the top with the milk chocolate curls.

# Chocolate Cream Roll

Preheat the oven to 350°. Line a 12-by-17-inch jelly-roll pan with foil. Butter and flour the foil.

**MAKE THE CAKE:** In a double boiler, melt the chocolate over hot, not simmering, water. Set aside to cool slightly.

In a medium bowl with an electric mixer, beat the egg yolks and granulated sugar until light and lemon-colored, about 5 minutes. Blend in the chocolate and vanilla. Set aside.

In a medium bowl, beat the egg whites until soft peaks form. Add the cream of tartar and beat until stiff peaks form. Stir one-fourth of the beaten whites into the chocolate mixture to lighten it. Gently but thoroughly fold in the remaining whites. Immediately transfer the batter to the prepared pan and smooth the top of the batter.

Bake for 15 minutes, or until the center of the cake springs back when lightly pressed. Cover the cake with a damp kitchen towel and cool to room temperature on a rack.

**PREPARE THE FILLING:** In a medium bowl, whip the cream with the confectioners' sugar and vanilla until stiff peaks form.

**TO ASSEMBLE:** Very gently lift the cake out of the pan along with the foil. Dust the top of the cake evenly with the cocoa. Spread the surface with the whipped cream, leaving a 1-inch border along the cake edges. With a long end toward you, roll up the cake, gently removing the foil as you go.

To serve, drizzle some of the Super Hot Fudge Sauce onto a plate and place a slice of the cake roll on top of the sauce. Serve any remaining sauce at the table.

CAKE
6 ounces semisweet chocolate, coarsely chopped
6 large eggs, separated
¼ cup granulated sugar
1 teaspoon vanilla extract
½ teaspoon cream of tartar

CREAM FILLING
1 cup heavy cream
2 tablespoons confectioners' sugar
1 teaspoon vanilla extract

2 teaspoons unsweetened cocoa powder
Super Hot Fudge Sauce (page 79)

YIELD: 12 servings

# Double-Fudge Chip Cake

❖

## CAKE
3 ounces unsweetened chocolate,
finely chopped
2¼ cups sifted cake flour
2 teaspoons baking soda
½ teaspoon salt
1 stick (½ cup) salted butter, softened
2¼ cups (packed) light brown sugar
3 large eggs, at room temperature
1½ teaspoons vanilla extract
1 cup sour cream
1 cup boiling water

## FROSTING
8 ounces unsweetened chocolate,
finely chopped
2 sticks (1 cup) unsalted butter,
softened
2 pounds confectioners' sugar
1 cup heavy cream
4 teaspoons vanilla extract
6 ounces milk chocolate chips (1 cup)

1 package chocolate kisses, for garnish

YIELD: *One 9-inch layer cake*

Preheat the oven to 350°. Butter and flour three 9-inch cake pans.

MAKE THE CAKE: In a double boiler, melt the chocolate over hot, not simmering, water. Set aside to cool.

In a medium bowl, whisk together the flour, baking soda, and salt.

In a large bowl with an electric mixer, cream the butter. Add the brown sugar and then the eggs, one at a time, blending well after each addition. Beat at high speed for 5 minutes. Beat in the vanilla and the melted chocolate.

Beat in the flour mixture alternately with the sour cream in 4 portions, beginning and ending with the flour mixture; beat well after each addition.

Stir in the boiling water and pour the batter at once into the prepared pans. Bake for 35 minutes, or until the center springs back when touched lightly. Set the cake pans on a rack to cool for 10 minutes. Then invert the cakes onto the racks to cool completely.

PREPARE THE FROSTING: In a double boiler, melt the chocolate with the butter. Set aside to cool to room temperature.

In a medium bowl with an electric mixer, blend the confectioners' sugar, cream, and vanilla until smooth. Add the cooled chocolate mixture and mix at low speed until blended. Place the frosting in the refrigerator until thick and firm yet still easy to spread, 20 to 30 minutes.

TO ASSEMBLE: Place one cake layer upside down on a cake dish. Spread one-fourth of the frosting on top and sprinkle with ½ cup of the chips. Add a second cake layer upside down and frost with another one-fourth of the frosting and the remaining ½ cup chips. Add the top layer upside down and frost the top and sides of the cake with the remaining frosting. Garnish the cake with the chocolate kisses.

# Chocolate Fudge Layered Banana Cake

Preheat the oven to 350°. Butter a 12-by-17-inch jelly-roll pan. Line the pan with parchment or wax paper, then butter and flour the paper.

MAKE THE CAKE: In a small bowl, whisk together the flour, baking soda, and salt.

In a large bowl with an electric mixer, cream the butter and sugar. Add the eggs one at a time, beating well after each addition. Beat in the mashed bananas and the vanilla. Beat in the flour mixture and the chocolate chips until smooth. Pour the batter into the prepared pan and bake for 20 to 25 minutes, or until the center is set. Cool on a rack to room temperature.

Loosen the cake with a spatula and carefully invert onto a large piece of foil. Cut the cake lengthwise into two pieces 5 by 15 inches, trimming off the outside edges of the cake.

PREPARE THE GANACHE FILLING: In a heavy medium saucepan, bring the cream to a simmer. Remove from the heat and stir in the sour cream. Pour the mixture over the chocolate in a medium bowl, then stir until smooth. Refrigerate until the filling firms up but is still spreadable.

Spread the ganache filling over one cake layer. Slice the 2 whole bananas into ¼-inch slices and arrange evenly over the ganache. Place the second cake layer on top.

MAKE THE GLAZE: In a heavy medium saucepan, bring the cream to a simmer. Remove from the heat and stir in the butter and chocolate. Stir until smooth.

Pour the warm glaze over the cake and smooth, allowing it to run down the sides. Place the cake in the freezer to firm for 30 to 40 minutes. Cut the cake crosswise into 8 slices and let sit at room temperature for 15 minutes before serving.

## CAKE
2½ cups cake flour, sifted
2 teaspoons baking soda
½ teaspoon salt
1½ sticks (¾ cup) unsalted butter, softened
1¾ cups sugar
4 large eggs
2½ cups mashed bananas plus 2 whole bananas
1 teaspoon vanilla extract
½ cup mini semisweet chocolate chips

## GANACHE FILLING
½ cup heavy cream
¼ cup sour cream
9 ounces semisweet chocolate, finely chopped

## CHOCOLATE GLAZE
½ cup heavy cream
1 tablespoon unsalted butter
6 ounces semisweet chocolate, finely chopped

YIELD: 8 servings

# White Chocolate Cheesecake

### CRUST
*1½ cups ladyfinger crumbs*
*4 ounces white chocolate, coarsely chopped*
*5 tablespoons unsalted butter, melted*

### FILLING
*18 ounces white chocolate*
*¼ cup heavy cream*
*1½ pounds cream cheese, softened*
*½ cup sugar*
*½ cup sour cream*
*4 large eggs*
*1 tablespoon vanilla extract*

### WHITE CHOCOLATE GANACHE
*8 ounces white chocolate, finely chopped*
*½ cup heavy cream*
*1 tablespoon unsalted butter*

*Fresh raspberries, for garnish*
*Raspberry Sauce (page 66)*

YIELD: *12 to 16 servings*

MAKE THE CRUST: In a food processor or blender, combine the ladyfinger crumbs and the white chocolate and process until the chocolate is finely chopped. Blend in the butter. Wrap the outside of a 9-inch springform pan in aluminum foil. Press the crust into the bottom and up the sides of the pan. Chill the crust.

Preheat the oven to 275°. Set a shallow baking pan filled with hot water on the bottom rack of the oven.

PREPARE THE FILLING: In a double boiler, melt the white chocolate with the cream over hot, not simmering, water. Set aside to cool slightly.

In a large bowl, beat the cream cheese and sugar until smooth. Beat in the sour cream, eggs, and vanilla. Beat in the white chocolate cream. Pour into the prepared pan.

Set the cheesecake on the center rack and bake for 1 hour. Reduce the heat to 250° and bake for 1 hour longer. Without opening the oven, turn off the heat but leave the cake in the oven for 1 hour. Cool the cheesecake on a rack for 30 minutes.

MEANWHILE, MAKE THE GANACHE: Place the white chocolate in a medium bowl. In a small saucepan, bring the cream and butter to a simmer. Pour the hot cream over the chocolate. Let stand, covered, for 5 minutes, then stir until smooth. Let the ganache cool to room temperature.

Pour the ganache over the cheesecake and spread it smooth. Cover the cheesecake and refrigerate for at least 8 hours or overnight.

To unmold, wrap a hot wet towel around the pan, then remove the sides of the springform. Garnish the cheesecake with fresh raspberries. Cut into wedges and serve with the Raspberry Sauce.

# Debbi's Deadly Chocolate Muffins

Preheat the oven to 350°. Lightly oil the top surface of a 12-cup muffin tin. Line the cups with paper liners.

In a double boiler, melt the chopped semisweet chocolate with the butter and stir until smooth. Remove from the heat and stir in the sour cream.

In a small bowl, whisk together the flour, baking soda, and salt.

In a large bowl with an electric mixer, beat the eggs and sugar until light and pale, about 5 minutes. Beat in the chocolate mixture and the vanilla. Add the flour mixture and 1 cup of the semisweet chocolate chips.

Spoon the batter evenly into the prepared muffin cups. Top with the remaining ¼ cup semisweet chips, the macadamia nuts, and the white chocolate chips. Bake for 20 to 25 minutes, or until the centers are set.

Set the muffin tin on a wire rack to cool for 15 minutes. Then remove the muffins to cool completely.

*12 ounces semisweet chocolate, coarsely chopped*
*1 stick (½ cup) unsalted butter*
*½ cup sour cream*
*1 cup sifted cake flour*
*½ teaspoon baking soda*
*¼ teaspoon salt*
*4 large eggs*
*½ cup (packed) light brown sugar*
*1 teaspoon vanilla extract*
*1¼ cups semisweet chocolate chips*
*¼ cup coarsely chopped macadamia nuts*
*¼ cup white chocolate chips*

YIELD: *12 muffins*

*Top the muffin batter with semisweet and white chocolate chips and chopped macadamia nuts.*

# Chocolate Chip Banana Bread

3 cups all-purpose flour
2 teaspoons baking powder
1 teaspoon salt
1½ sticks (¾ cup) unsalted butter,
softened
2 cups sugar
3 cups mashed bananas (about 8)
4 large eggs, well beaten
2 teaspoons vanilla extract
1 cup mini semisweet chocolate chips

YIELD: *Two 9-inch loaves*

Preheat the oven to 350°. Lightly butter two 9-by-5-inch loaf pans. Line the bottoms with buttered parchment or wax paper.

In a bowl, whisk together the flour, baking soda, and salt.

In a medium bowl, cream the butter and sugar. Add the bananas and eggs, beating until well blended. Beat in the vanilla.

Add the dry ingredients to the banana mixture and blend well. Stir in the chocolate chips. Do not overmix.

Pour the batter into the prepared pans and bake for 55 to 60 minutes, or until golden brown and a cake tester inserted in the center comes out clean. Set the pans on a rack to cool for 15 minutes. Then turn out of the pans to cool completely.

# Chocolate-Toffee Speckled Cake

Preheat the oven to 350°. Butter two 9-inch cake pans. Line the bottoms with circles of wax paper, then butter and flour the paper.

MAKE THE CAKE: In a medium bowl, whisk together the flour, baking powder, baking soda, and salt.

In a medium bowl with an electric mixer, cream the butter and sugar. Beat in the sour cream. Beat in the yolks one at a time. Beat in the vanilla. In three additions, alternately stir in the flour mixture and the milk, beating well after each addition. Fold in the semisweet chocolate.

Spread the batter in the prepared pans and bake for 30 to 35 minutes, or until a cake tester inserted in the center comes out clean. Cool the cakes in the pans on a rack for 20 minutes. Then invert the cakes onto the racks to cool completely.

MEANWHILE, MAKE THE GANACHE: Place the milk chocolate in a medium bowl. In a small saucepan, bring the cream to a boil. Pour over the chocolate. Let stand, covered, for 5 minutes, then stir until smooth. Chill in the refrigerator for 1 hour.

TO ASSEMBLE: With an electric mixer, slowly beat the ganache until thickened and smooth; be careful not to overbeat or the ganache will separate.

Spread 1½ cups of the ganache over the bottom cake layer. Sprinkle with half of the chopped toffee. Top with the second cake layer. Frost with the remaining ganache. Sprinkle the top of the cake with the remaining toffee. Refrigerate until ready to serve.

## CAKE
*3 cups sifted cake flour*
*1¼ teaspoons baking powder*
*½ teaspoon baking soda*
*½ teaspoon salt*
*1 stick (½ cup) unsalted butter, softened*
*1½ cups (packed) light brown sugar*
*¼ cup sour cream*
*6 large egg yolks*
*2 teaspoons vanilla extract*
*¾ cup plus 2 tablespoons milk, at room temperature*
*6 ounces semisweet chocolate, finely grated*

## CHOCOLATE GANACHE
*18 ounces milk chocolate, finely chopped*
*1½ cups heavy cream*

*1 cup chopped chocolate-covered toffee*

YIELD: *One 9-inch layer cake*

# Black and White Cupcakes

## CREAM CHEESE LAYER

*8 ounces cream cheese, softened*
*¼ cup sugar*
*1 large egg*

## CAKE LAYER

*1½ cups all-purpose flour*
*1 cup sugar*
*¼ cup plus 1 tablespoon unsweetened cocoa powder*
*1 teaspoon baking soda*
*½ teaspoon salt*
*½ cup water*
*⅓ cup vegetable oil*
*1 large egg*
*1 teaspoon vanilla extract*
*3 ounces semisweet chocolate chips (½ cup)*

YIELD: *12 cupcakes*

Preheat the oven to 350°. Line 12 muffin cups with foil or paper muffin cup liners.

PREPARE THE CREAM CHEESE LAYER: In a medium bowl, beat the cream cheese until smooth. Beat in the sugar and egg until well blended.

MAKE THE CAKE LAYER: In a large bowl, whisk together the flour, sugar, cocoa, baking soda, and salt. In a small bowl, beat the water, oil, egg, and vanilla. Add to the flour mixture and stir until just combined. Stir in half of the chocolate chips.

Fill the muffin cups about half full with the chocolate cake batter. Using the remaining cake batter and all of the cream cheese batter, spoon equal amounts on top of the cake batter, creating a top that is half chocolate and half cream cheese. Sprinkle the tops of the cupcakes with the remaining chocolate chips.

Bake for 30 to 35 minutes, or until a cake tester inserted into the center comes out clean. Set the muffin tin on a wire rack to cool for 10 minutes. Turn the cupcakes out of the pan to cool completely.

*After filling the muffin cups half full with the chocolate cake batter, spoon on the remaining chocolate batter and all of the cream cheese batter to create a top that is half dark and half light.*

# Coconut Almond Cake

Preheat the oven to 350°. Butter a 9-inch cake pan. Line the bottom with a circle of wax paper, then butter and flour the paper.

**MAKE THE CAKE:** In a small bowl, whisk together the flour, baking soda, and salt.

In a medium bowl with an electric mixer, cream the butter, granulated sugar, and almond paste. Beat in the eggs one at a time, beating well after each addition. Beat in the vanilla and almond extracts. Stir in the coconut.

In three additions, alternately stir in the flour mixture and the milk, beating well after each addition.

Pour the batter into the prepared pan. Bake for 45 to 50 minutes, or until a cake tester inserted in the center comes out clean. Set the cake pan on a wire rack to cool for 20 minutes. Then invert the cake onto the rack to cool completely.

**MEANWHILE, MAKE THE FUDGE FILLING:** In a small saucepan, melt the butter with the coconut cream. Remove from the heat and stir in the unsweetened chocolate and 1½ ounces of the semisweet chocolate. Stir until melted and smooth.

Beat in the cream cheese and coconut. Let cool slightly, then stir in the remaining 2 ounces chopped semisweet chocolate. Cool the filling until firm but still spreadable.

**TO ASSEMBLE:** With a serrated knife, cut the cake horizontally into two layers. Place one layer cut-side up and spread with the cooled fudge filling. Top with the second layer.

**MAKE THE TOPPING:** In a large bowl, beat the cream with the confectioners' sugar and vanilla until soft peaks form. Spread the whipped cream over the cake and sprinkle with the toasted coconut. Serve immediately.

### CAKE
*1½ cups all-purpose flour*
*½ teaspoon baking soda*
*¼ teaspoon salt*
*1 stick (½ cup) unsalted butter*
*1¼ cups granulated sugar*
*3 ounces almond paste (about ⅓ cup)*
*3 large eggs*
*1 teaspoon vanilla extract*
*¼ teaspoon almond extract*
*½ cup shredded coconut*
*½ cup milk*

### FUDGE FILLING
*6 tablespoons unsalted butter*
*½ cup sweetened coconut cream*
*1½ ounces unsweetened chocolate, coarsely chopped*
*3½ ounces semisweet chocolate, coarsely chopped*
*1 ounce cream cheese, softened*
*¾ cup shredded coconut*

### TOPPING
*1½ cups heavy cream*
*3 tablespoons confectioners' sugar*
*1½ teaspoons vanilla extract*
*¼ cup shredded coconut, toasted*

**YIELD:** *One 9-inch layer cake*

# Ganache-Filled Devil's Food Cake

### CAKE

1¾ cups boiling water
6 ounces semisweet chocolate, coarsely chopped
1 cup unsweetened cocoa powder
2 cups sifted cake flour
2 teaspoons baking soda
¼ teaspoon salt
10 ounces unsalted butter, softened
1¾ cups (packed) dark brown sugar
4 large eggs
2 teaspoons vanilla extract

### CHOCOLATE GANACHE

½ cup heavy cream
2 tablespoons unsalted butter
4 ounces semisweet chocolate, finely chopped

### CHOCOLATE FROSTING

2½ sticks (1¼ cups) plus 2 tablespoons unsalted butter, softened
4½ cups confectioners' sugar
1 cup unsweetened cocoa powder
2 teaspoons vanilla extract
¼ cup plus 2 tablespoons milk

YIELD: *One 9-inch layer cake*

MAKE THE CAKE: Preheat the oven to 350°. Butter two 9-inch cake pans. Line the bottoms with circles of wax paper, then butter and flour the paper.

In a medium bowl, pour the boiling water over the chopped chocolate. Set aside for 5 minutes. Add the cocoa and stir until the mixture is smooth. Set aside to cool to room temperature.

In a small bowl, whisk together the flour, baking soda, and salt.

In a large bowl with an electric mixer, cream the butter and brown sugar. Add the eggs one at a time, beating well after each addition. Beat in the vanilla. Add the flour mixture and half of the chocolate mixture. Beat on low speed to combine, then on high for 1½ minutes. Add the remaining chocolate mixture and beat on low speed to combine.

Pour the batter into the prepared pans and bake for 30 to 40 minutes, or until a cake tester inserted in the center comes out clean. Set the cake pans on a wire rack to cool for 20 minutes. Then invert the cakes onto the racks to cool completely.

PREPARE THE GANACHE: In a small saucepan, bring the cream and butter to a simmer. Add the chocolate, cover for 5 minutes, then stir until smooth. Refrigerate the ganache until firm enough to spread.

MEANWHILE, MAKE THE FROSTING: In a large bowl with an electric mixer, cream the butter. In a medium bowl, whisk together the sugar and cocoa. Beat one-third of the sugar-cocoa mixture into the butter. Mix in the vanilla. Add the rest of the sugar-cocoa mixture alternately with the milk and beat until the frosting is smooth.

ASSEMBLE THE CAKE: Top one cake layer with the ganache. Add the second layer of cake and frost the sides of the cake, then the top. Decoratively pipe frosting around the base and top edges of the cake.

# *Skinny Fallen Mousse Cake with Berry Sauce*

MAKE THE CAKE: Preheat the oven to 375°. Line the bottom of an 8½-inch springform pan with a circle of wax paper. Lightly spray the wax paper and sides of the pan with nonstick cooking spray.

In a food processor, grind the toasted almonds for 2 to 3 seconds, or just until ground; do not overprocess or the nuts will be oily.

In a double boiler, blend ½ cup of the sugar with the cocoa and 2 tablespoons of the boiling water. Add the 3 remaining tablespoons boiling water and stir until smooth. Add the sweet chocolate and stir over hot, not simmering, water, until the chocolate is melted. Stir in the vanilla, remove from the heat, and set aside.

In a small bowl, beat the egg yolks until thick and pale. Whisk about ¼ cup of the chocolate mixture into the eggs to warm them. Transfer the warmed eggs to the chocolate mixture and stir to combine. Stir in the flour and ground almonds and set aside.

In a large bowl, beat the 4 egg whites until foamy. Add the cream of tartar and beat until soft peaks form. Add the remaining ¼ cup sugar and beat until stiff peaks form.

Stir one-fourth of the egg whites into the chocolate mixture to lighten it, then gently but thoroughly fold in the remaining egg whites. Spread the batter in the prepared pan and bake for 25 minutes, or until a cake tester inserted in the center comes out clean. Set the pan on a wire rack to cool completely.

MAKE THE SAUCE: In a food processor, purée 2 cups of the strawberries and 1 cup of the raspberries. Strain through a fine-mesh sieve to remove the seeds. Slice the remaining 1 cup strawberries and stir the sliced strawberries and remaining raspberries into the strained purée.

To serve, remove the sides of the pan. Dust with confectioners' sugar, cut into 12 wedges, and serve the berry sauce on the side.

### CAKE
*¼ cup whole almonds, toasted*
*¾ cup sugar*
*½ cup unsweetened cocoa powder, sifted*
*5 tablespoons boiling water*
*2 ounces sweet chocolate, finely chopped*
*1 teaspoon vanilla extract*
*2 large eggs, separated, plus 2 egg whites*
*3 tablespoons all-purpose flour*
*¼ teaspoon cream of tartar*

### BERRY SAUCE
*3 cups whole strawberries*
*2 cups raspberries*

*Confectioners' sugar, for dusting*

YIELD: *12 servings*

# "Light" Chocolate Cheesecake

## CRUST
1 cup chocolate wafer cookie crumbs
2 tablespoons granulated sugar
1 tablespoon water

## FILLING
1 cup (packed) dark brown sugar
¼ cup unsweetened cocoa powder
¼ cup all-purpose flour
16 ounces nonfat cream cheese
1 cup light sour cream
4 large egg whites
1½ ounces German sweet chocolate,
melted and cooled
2 teaspoons vanilla extract

YIELD: *10 servings*

Preheat the oven to 300°. Spray the sides and bottom of an 8½-inch springform pan with nonstick cooking spray. Place a shallow roasting pan of water on the bottom rack of the oven.

**PREPARE THE CRUST:** In a medium bowl, use your fingers or a fork to toss the cookie crumbs with the granulated sugar and water until evenly moistened. Press the crumb mixture into the bottom and one-third of the way up the sides of the springform pan.

**MAKE THE FILLING:** In a small bowl, blend the brown sugar, cocoa, and flour. In a food processor, process the cream cheese and flour-cocoa mixture until smooth. Add the sour cream and blend until smooth. Add the egg whites and blend. Add the melted chocolate and vanilla and blend.

Pour the filling into the crust and place the cheesecake on the center rack of the oven. Bake for 1 hour, or until the filling is just set (it will still be wobbly in the center). Turn off the heat but leave the cake in the oven for another 30 minutes. Remove from the oven and cool in the pan on a wire rack. Cover and refrigerate until well chilled, at least 8 hours or overnight.

To serve, run a knife around the edges of the cake to loosen it from the side of the springform, then remove the sides of the pan.

# Pies & Pastries

# Mousse-Filled Cookie Pie

### CRUST

1¼ cups all-purpose flour
¼ cup unsweetened cocoa powder
½ teaspoon baking soda
1 stick (½ cup) unsalted butter
½ cup (packed) light brown sugar
¼ cup granulated sugar
1 large egg, at room temperature
1 cup mini semisweet chocolate chips

### MOUSSE FILLING

2 cups heavy cream
2 teaspoons unflavored gelatin
8 ounces white chocolate, coarsely chopped
1 teaspoon almond extract

Large white and dark Chocolate Scrolls (page 101), for garnish

YIELD: *One 9-inch pie*

Preheat the oven to 350°. Lightly butter a 9-inch pie plate.

MAKE THE CRUST: In a small bowl, whisk together the flour, cocoa powder, and baking soda.

In medium bowl with an electric mixer, cream the butter with the brown and granulated sugars. Beat in the egg. On low speed, gradually beat in the flour mixture until just combined. Stir in the chocolate chips.

Press the dough evenly into the prepared pie plate and chill in the refrigerator for 15 minutes. Bake for 15 to 20 minutes, or just until set. Set aside to cool to room temperature.

MEANWHILE, MAKE THE MOUSSE FILLING: Place ¼ cup of the cream in a small bowl. Sprinkle the gelatin on top and let stand for 5 minutes to soften.

Place the white chocolate in a medium bowl. In a medium saucepan, bring 1 cup of the cream to a simmer. Pour the hot cream over the chocolate. Let stand, covered, for 5 minutes, then stir until smooth. Whisk in the softened gelatin and almond extract. Set aside to cool to lukewarm.

In a medium bowl, beat the remaining ¾ cup cream until soft peaks form. Gently whisk about ½ cup of the whipped cream into the chocolate mixture to lighten it. Gently but thoroughly fold in the remaining whipped cream. Spoon the mousse filling into the crust. Refrigerate the pie for at least 3 hours to set.

Serve garnished with large white and dark Chocolate Scrolls.

# Chocolate Angel Pie

Preheat the oven to 275°.

MAKE THE MERINGUE SHELL: In a medium bowl, beat the egg whites, salt, and cream of tartar until foamy. Gradually add the sugar and beat until stiff, glossy peaks form. Spread the meringue over the bottom and up the sides of a 9-inch pie plate. Build the meringue up around the rim, extending it 1 inch higher than the rim.

Sprinkle the chopped hazelnuts over the bottom of the crust. Bake for 35 minutes, or until the meringue is dry and light golden. Let the meringue shell stand in the oven with the heat turned off and the door ajar for 1 hour.

MEANWHILE, MAKE THE FILLING: In a medium saucepan, combine the sugar, cornstarch, and salt. Stir in the milk until well blended. Bring the mixture to a boil over medium heat, stirring constantly. Boil, stirring, for 1 minute. Remove the pan from the heat. Add the chocolate and stir until melted and smooth. Transfer the mixture to a bowl; cool to room temperature.

In a medium bowl, beat the cream until stiff peaks form. Gently and thoroughly fold the cream into the chocolate mixture. Spoon the filling into the meringue shell. Refrigerate the pie for about 30 minutes before serving.

Garnish the pie with chocolate shavings and whole hazelnuts dusted with confectioners' sugar.

## MERINGUE SHELL
*4 large egg whites*
*¼ teaspoon salt*
*¼ teaspoon cream of tartar*
*1 cup sugar*
*⅓ cup hazelnuts—toasted, skinned and finely chopped*

## FILLING
*¼ cup sugar*
*3 tablespoons cornstarch*
*½ teaspoon salt*
*1½ cups milk*
*6 ounces semisweet chocolate, finely chopped*
*1¼ cups heavy cream*

*Chocolate shavings, whole hazelnuts, and confectioners' sugar, for garnish*

YIELD: *One 9-inch pie*

# Caramel Fudge Mac Tart

### PASTRY
*½ cup macadamia nuts*
*¼ cup sugar*
*¾ cup all-purpose flour*
*4 tablespoons cold unsalted butter*
*1 egg yolk*
*1 tablespoon water*
*1 teaspoon vanilla extract*

### CARAMEL LAYER
*¾ cup sugar*
*¼ cup water*
*½ cup heavy cream, scalded*
*2 tablespoons unsalted butter, at room temperature*

### CHOCOLATE FUDGE LAYER
*½ cup heavy cream*
*1 egg yolk*
*1 tablespoon sugar*
*3 tablespoons sour cream*
*6 ounces semisweet chocolate, finely chopped*
*1 teaspoon vanilla extract*

*Chopped toasted macadamia nuts, for garnish*

YIELD: *One 9-inch tart*

MAKE THE PASTRY: In a food processor, grind the macadamia nuts with the sugar into small pieces. Add the flour and butter, then process until the dough resembles coarse meal. In a small bowl, lightly beat the egg yolk with the water and vanilla. With the machine running, add the egg yolk mixture and process until the dough gathers into a ball.

Lightly butter a 9-inch tart pan with a removable bottom. Scrape the dough into the pan and press into the bottom and up the sides. Cover and refrigerate for 30 minutes.

MEANWHILE, MAKE THE CARAMEL LAYER: In a small heavy saucepan, dissolve the sugar in the water over low heat, stirring constantly. Bring to a boil over medium-high heat, then let boil without stirring until the syrup turns a light amber. While the syrup is boiling, brush down the sides of the pan from time to time with a wet pastry brush to prevent crystals from forming. Remove the pan from the heat and stir in the hot cream (be careful, it will bubble rapidly). Continue stirring, over low heat if necessary, until all of the caramel is dissolved into the cream. Stir in the butter and set aside to cool to room temperature.

Preheat the oven to 350°. Prick the tart dough all over with a fork and bake for 18 minutes, or until the crust is golden. Cool to room temperature.

MEANWHILE, MAKE THE CHOCOLATE FUDGE LAYER: In a heavy medium saucepan, stir together the cream, egg yolk, sugar, and sour cream over medium heat. Stir lightly until the mixture just begins to scald. Remove from the heat, stir in the chocolate and vanilla, and blend until smooth. Pour the fudge into the cooled crust.

Pour three-fourths of the cooled caramel over the fudge layer. Top the caramel layer with chopped macadamia nuts. Drizzle the remaining caramel over the nuts.

Cover the tart and chill in the refrigerator to set. Let the tart sit at room temperature for 20 minutes before serving.

# Glazed Honey-Nut Rolls

PREPARE THE FILLING: In a small saucepan, combine the honey, water, lemon juice, and cinnamon. Simmer for 10 minutes. Keep warm.

In a medium bowl, combine the walnuts, raisins, vanilla, almond extract, and ½ cup of the honey mixture. Stir in the chocolate chips and set aside.

TO ASSEMBLE AND BAKE: Preheat the oven to 375°. Keeping the rest of the phyllo covered with plastic wrap and a damp towel, lay a sheet of dough on a work surface. Cut in half crosswise. Brush each half with melted butter. With a short end facing you, spoon about 1½ tablespoons of filling onto the phyllo. Fold in the sides and roll up the dough. Brush the rolls with more butter and place on a cookie sheet. Repeat with the remaining dough, filling, and butter. Bake for 20 minutes, or until golden. Transfer to wire racks to cool, but immediately brush the rolls with the remaining honey glaze.

MAKE THE CHOCOLATE GLAZE: In a small saucepan, bring the cream to a simmer. Remove from the heat, add the chips, and let stand for 5 minutes; stir until smooth. Let cool, then drizzle over the nut rolls. Dust the rolls with confectioners' sugar.

### FILLING AND HONEY GLAZE
¾ cup clover honey
⅓ cup water
1 teaspoon fresh lemon juice
1 cinnamon stick
8 ounces walnuts, coarsely chopped
¾ cup raisins (4 ounces)
1 teaspoon vanilla extract
¼ teaspoon almond extract
6 ounces semisweet chocolate chips
(about 1 cup)

### ASSEMBLY
10 sheets (13 by 22 inches) frozen phyllo dough (about ¼ pound), thawed
1 stick (½ cup) unsalted butter, melted

### CHOCOLATE GLAZE
⅓ cup heavy cream
4 ounces semisweet chocolate chips

Confectioners' sugar, for dusting

YIELD: *20 nut rolls*

*With a short end of the phyllo facing you, place about 1½ tablespoons of the filling about 1 inch in from the end. Fold in the sides of the dough and roll up.*

# Chocolate Mousse Tart

## CRUST

*1 large egg yolk*
*2 tablespoons ice water*
*1 teaspoon vanilla extract*
*1¼ cups all-purpose flour*
*¼ cup sugar*
*6 tablespoons cold unsalted butter,*
*cut into pieces*

## FILLING

*3 ounces coarsely chopped semisweet*
*chocolate plus 9 ounces finely*
*chopped semisweet chocolate*
*2 cups heavy cream*
*¼ cup confectioners' sugar*
*1 teaspoon vanilla extract*

*Whipped cream and Chocolate*
*Scrolls (page 101), for garnish*

**YIELD:** *8 servings*

**MAKE THE CRUST:** In a small bowl, combine the egg yolk, water, and vanilla. In a medium bowl, whisk together the flour and sugar.

Cut the butter into the flour-sugar mixture until it resembles coarse meal. Stir in the egg yolk mixture. If the dough does not mass together, add up to 1 more tablespoon water, a bit at a time. Shape the dough into a disk, wrap in plastic, and chill for 1 hour.

Preheat the oven to 400°. Remove the dough from the refrigerator and let stand for 10 minutes, then roll it into an 11-inch round. Fit it into a 9-inch tart pan with a removable bottom. Freeze the tart shell for 15 minutes.

Prick the tart shell in several places with a fork. Line the shell with aluminum foil and fill with dried beans, rice, or metal pie weights and then bake for 5 minutes. Remove the foil and weights, and bake for 15 minutes longer, or until golden brown. Set the tart shell on a wire rack to cool to room temperature.

**MAKE THE FILLING:** In a double boiler, melt the 3 ounces of coarsely chopped chocolate over hot, not simmering, water. Pour the melted chocolate into the bottom of the cooled crust; chill while you make the mousse.

In a small saucepan, bring ½ cup of the cream to a simmer. Remove the pan from the heat and stir in 6 ounces of the finely chopped chocolate. Cover and set aside for 5 minutes, then stir the mixture until smooth. Transfer the chocolate cream to a large bowl.

In another large bowl, whip the remaining 1½ cups cream with the confectioners' sugar and vanilla until soft peaks form. Fold one-third of the cream into the chocolate mixture to lighten it. Stir in the remaining 3 ounces chopped chocolate, then gently fold in the remaining whipped cream.

**TO ASSEMBLE:** Spread the mousse evenly in the tart shell. Chill until serving time. Garnish with whipped cream and Chocolate Scrolls.

# Double-Chocolate Silk Pie

❖

MAKE THE CRUST: In a medium bowl, combine the crumbs and melted butter. Press the crumb mixture into the bottom and up the sides of a 9-inch pie plate. Chill the pie crust while you make the filling.

PREPARE THE FILLING: In a double boiler, scald the cream; stir in the sugar and salt. In a small bowl, lightly beat the yolks. Whisk about ¼ cup of the hot cream into the yolks to warm them. Transfer the warmed eggs to the double boiler and cook over simmering water, whisking constantly, until the custard just begins to thicken and coats the back of a spoon, 8 to 9 minutes. Remove from the heat and add the chocolate and vanilla. Stir until the chocolate melts and the custard is smooth.

Pour the custard filling into the pie crust. Cool to room temperature. Place a piece of plastic wrap directly on the filling to prevent a skin from forming. Refrigerate the pie overnight to set the filling. Remove the plastic wrap and smooth the top of the pie. Garnish with Chocolate Scrolls and rosettes of whipped cream.

### CRUST
*1½ cups chocolate wafer crumbs*
*6 tablespoons unsalted butter, melted*

### FILLING
*1½ cups heavy cream*
*3 tablespoons sugar*
*Pinch of salt*
*5 large egg yolks*
*10 ounces semisweet chocolate, finely chopped*
*1½ teaspoons vanilla extract*

*Chocolate Scrolls (page 101) and whipped cream, for garnish*

YIELD: *One 9-inch pie*

*To prevent a skin from forming on the pie filling, place a sheet of plastic wrap directly on its surface.*

# Chocolate Coconut Pecan Pie

### CRUST
*1 cup all-purpose flour*
*⅛ teaspoon salt*
*6 tablespoons cold unsalted butter,*
*cut into pieces*
*2 to 3 tablespoons ice water*

### FILLING AND TOPPING
*2 tablespoons all-purpose flour*
*¼ teaspoon baking powder*
*¼ teaspoon salt*
*4 tablespoons (¼ cup) unsalted*
*butter*
*¾ cup (packed) light brown sugar*
*4 large egg yolks*
*2 teaspoons vanilla extract*
*1 cup shredded coconut*
*1 cup coarsely chopped pecans*
*4 ounces semisweet chocolate, coarsely*
*chopped*
*¾ cup heavy cream*

*Whole pecans and whipped cream,*
*for garnish*

### YIELD: *One 9-inch pie*

MAKE THE CRUST: In a small bowl, whisk together the flour and salt. With a pastry blender, incorporate the butter into the flour until the mixture resembles coarse meal. Toss the mixture with a fork, sprinkling on just enough of the ice water to form a cohesive dough. Flatten the dough into a disk, wrap in plastic wrap, and chill in the refrigerator for 30 minutes. Roll out to a 12-inch circle and fit into a 9-inch pie plate. Trim and crimp the edges. Return to the refrigerator while you make the filling.

Preheat the oven to 350°.

PREPARE THE FILLING: In a small bowl, whisk together the flour, baking powder, and salt. In a medium bowl with an electric mixer, cream the butter and sugar. Beat in the egg yolks and the vanilla. Slowly beat in the flour mixture. Stir in the coconut, pecans, and half of the chopped chocolate. Blend in the cream until smooth.

Pour the filling into the pie crust and sprinkle with the remaining chopped chocolate. Bake for 40 to 45 minutes, or until the crust is golden brown. The center of the filling will still be a bit jiggly. Let cool to room temperature, then chill for 2 hours to set.

Garnish each slice of pie with a whole pecan and a whipped cream rosette.

# Peanut Butter Cream Pie

MAKE THE CRUST: In a double boiler, melt the 6 ounces of chocolate chips and butter over low heat. Remove from the heat and stir until smooth. Gently stir in the rice cereal until completely coated. Set aside to cool to lukewarm, then stir in the mini chips. Press into the bottom and up the sides of a buttered 9-inch pie plate. Chill for 30 minutes to set the chocolate.

PREPARE THE FILLING: In a large bowl with an electric mixer, beat the cream cheese until fluffy. Beat in the condensed milk, peanut butter, and vanilla.

In a medium bowl, beat the heavy cream until soft peaks form. Fold the whipped cream into the peanut butter mixture. Pour the filling into the crust.

MAKE THE TOPPING: In a double boiler, melt the milk chocolate over hot, not simmering, water. Add the heavy cream and stir constantly until blended. Set aside to cool slightly, then drizzle the chocolate over the top of the pie. Refrigerate until firm, about 2 hours. Garnish with milk chocolate curls.

## CHOCOLATE CRUST
*6 ounces semisweet chocolate chips
(about 1 cup)
5 tablespoons unsalted butter
2½ cups crisp rice cereal
¼ cup mini semisweet chocolate chips*

## FILLING
*8 ounces cream cheese, softened
One 14-ounce can sweetened
condensed milk
¾ cup creamy peanut butter
2 teaspoons vanilla extract
1 cup heavy cream*

## TOPPING
*3 ounces milk chocolate, finely
chopped
2 tablespoons heavy cream*

*Milk chocolate curls, for garnish*

YIELD: *One 9-inch pie*

*Use a spatula to fold whipped cream into the cream cheese-peanut butter mixture.*

# Chocolate Pumpkin Pie

### CRUST
6 tablespoons cold unsalted butter
1 cup all-purpose flour
¼ teaspoon salt
2 to 3 tablespoons ice water

### PUMPKIN FILLING
1 cup (packed) light brown sugar
1 tablespoon plus 1 teaspoon
all-purpose flour
1 teaspoon cinnamon
¼ teaspoon grated nutmeg
¼ teaspoon salt
½ teaspoon ground ginger
⅛ teaspoon ground cloves
1 large egg
1 large egg white
2 tablespoons vanilla extract
One 15-ounce can unsweetened solid-
pack pumpkin purée
1 cup light cream or half-and-half

### CHOCOLATE TOPPING
4 ounces semisweet chocolate, coarsely
chopped
½ cup heavy cream
2 tablespoons granulated sugar

YIELD: *One 9-inch pie*

MAKE THE CRUST: With a pastry blender, incorporate the butter into the flour until the mixture resembles coarse meal. Toss the mixture with a fork, sprinkling on just enough of the ice water to form a cohesive dough. Flatten the dough into a disk, wrap in plastic wrap, and chill in the refrigerator for 45 minutes. Roll out to an 11-inch circle and fit into a 9-inch pie plate. Trim and crimp the edges. Return to the refrigerator while you make the filling.

Preheat the oven to 350°.

PREPARE THE PUMPKIN FILLING: In a medium bowl with an electric mixer, beat the brown sugar, flour, cinnamon, nutmeg, salt, ginger, and cloves until well mixed. Beat in the egg, egg white, and vanilla until smooth. Beat in the pumpkin, then the light cream. Pour into the chilled pastry shell. Bake for 40 minutes, or until the center is set. Cool on a rack to room temperature.

MEANWHILE, MAKE THE CHOCOLATE TOPPING: Place the chocolate in a small bowl. In a small saucepan, bring the heavy cream and the granulated sugar to a simmer, then stir until the sugar is dissolved. Pour the hot cream over the chocolate. Let stand, covered, for 5 minutes, then stir until smooth. Chill the chocolate topping mixture until thickened but still pourable, about 30 minutes.

Pour the chocolate over the pumpkin layer and chill the pie until the chocolate is set, about 1 hour.

# Chocolate-Glazed Creamy Lemon Turnovers

**PREPARE THE PASTRY:** In a medium bowl, whisk together the flour, sugar, and salt. With a pastry blender, incorporate the butter and cream cheese until they are the size of small peas. With a fork, stir in the ice water. Gather the dough into a ball, flatten into a disk, wrap in plastic, and chill in the refrigerator for 30 minutes.

**MAKE THE LEMON FILLING:** In a double boiler, melt the butter. In a medium bowl, whisk together the egg yolks, egg, sugar, lemon juice, and lemon peel. Add the egg mixture to the butter and cook, stirring frequently, until the mixture thickens and heavily coats the back of a spoon, about 15 minutes. Transfer the filling to a small bowl and refrigerate until firm, about 2 hours.

**TO BAKE:** Preheat the oven to 400°. Cut the chilled dough in half and return one half to the refrigerator. Roll the remaining half into a 12-by-16-inch rectangle. Cut into twelve 4-inch squares. Spoon about 1 tablespoon of filling into the center of each square. Moisten two adjacent sides of a pastry square with water, then fold the pastry over to form a triangle. Crimp the edges to seal. Brush each turnover with some of the beaten egg and cut three slits as steam vents. Sprinkle the tops with granulated sugar and place on an ungreased cookie sheet. Bake for 20 minutes, or until golden. Place on a rack to cool to room temperature. Repeat with the remaining dough and filling.

**MEANWHILE, MAKE THE CHOCOLATE GLAZE:** Place the chocolate chips in a small bowl. In a small saucepan, bring the cream to a simmer. Pour the hot cream over the chocolate. Let stand, covered, for 5 minutes, then stir until smooth.

Drizzle the turnovers with the chocolate glaze.

## PASTRY
*2 cups all-purpose flour*
*2 tablespoons sugar*
*½ teaspoon salt*
*1½ sticks (¾ cup) cold unsalted
butter, cut into pieces*
*2 ounces cold cream cheese, cut into
pieces*
*3 tablespoons ice water*

## LEMON FILLING
*6 tablespoons unsalted butter*
*4 large egg yolks*
*1 large egg*
*¾ cup sugar*
*¼ cup fresh lemon juice*
*2 teaspoons grated lemon peel*

## TOPPINGS
*1 egg, beaten*
*Granulated sugar, for sprinkling*
*5 ounces semisweet chocolate chips*
*½ cup heavy cream*

**YIELD:** *2 dozen turnovers*

# Chocolate Turtle Pie

## CRUST
1¼ cups graham cracker crumbs
4 tablespoons (¼ cup) unsalted
butter, melted
2 tablespoons sugar
3 ounces milk chocolate, finely
chopped

## FILLING
¾ cup sugar
3 tablespoons water
2 cups heavy cream, scalded
5 large egg yolks
6 ounces semisweet chocolate, finely
chopped
1 teaspoon vanilla extract
¼ cup chopped pecans
¼ cup semisweet chocolate chips

YIELD: *One 9-inch pie*

Preheat the oven to 350°.

MAKE THE CRUST: In a medium bowl, blend the graham cracker crumbs, butter, and sugar. Stir in the milk chocolate. Press the crust mixture into the bottom and up the sides of a 9-inch pie plate. Refrigerate until ready to use.

PREPARE THE FILLING: In a heavy medium saucepan, dissolve the sugar in the water over low heat, stirring constantly. Bring to a boil over medium-high heat, then let boil without stirring until the syrup turns a light amber. While the syrup is boiling, brush down the sides of the pan from time to time with a wet pastry brush to prevent crystals from forming. Remove the pan from the heat and stir in the hot cream (be careful, it will bubble rapidly). Continue stirring, over heat if necessary, until all of the caramel is dissolved into the cream.

In a medium bowl, lightly beat the egg yolks. Whisk about ½ cup of the hot caramel cream into the eggs to warm them. Transfer the warmed eggs to the caramel cream in the saucepan. Stir in the chopped semisweet chocolate and the vanilla, stirring until melted and smooth.

Pour the filling mixture into the pie crust. Sprinkle the pecans and chocolate chips on top. Bake for about 35 minutes, or until the center is just set. Transfer to a wire rack to cool completely, then refrigerate until firm, about 4 hours.

# Milk Chocolate Toffee Cream Pie

Preheat the oven to 350°.

MAKE THE CRUST: In a medium bowl, combine the cookie crumbs, butter, and sugar. Press the mixture into the bottom and up the sides of a 9-inch pie plate. Bake for 10 minutes. Place on a wire rack to cool.

PREPARE THE FILLING: Place the chocolate in a small bowl. In a small saucepan, bring ½ cup of the cream to a simmer. Pour the hot cream over the chocolate. Let stand, covered, for 5 minutes, then stir until smooth.

In a medium bowl with an electric mixer, beat the cream cheese, sugar, and vanilla until smooth. Beat in the remaining ¼ cup cream. Gently beat in the cooled chocolate mixture. Fold in ½ cup of the chopped toffee candy.

Pour the filling into the cooled crust, sprinkle with the remaining ¼ cup chopped toffee, and chill until firm, about 2 hours.

### CRUST
*1½ cups chocolate wafer crumbs*
*5 tablespoons unsalted butter, melted*
*2 tablespoons granulated sugar*

### FILLING
*6 ounces milk chocolate, coarsely chopped*
*¾ cup heavy cream*
*8 ounces cream cheese, softened*
*¼ cup (packed) light brown sugar*
*1 tablespoon vanilla extract*
*¾ cup chopped chocolate-covered toffee candy*

YIELD: *One 9-inch pie*

*Use your fingers to shape a layer of the wafer crumb mixture over the bottom and sides of a 9-inch pie plate.*

# Chocolate Banana Cream Pie

## CRUST
1 cup all-purpose flour
2 tablespoons sugar
½ teaspoon salt
6 tablespoons cold unsalted butter,
cut into pieces
1 egg yolk
2 tablespoons ice water

## FILLING
¾ cup sugar
5 tablespoons cornstarch
¼ teaspoon salt
1½ cups heavy cream
1 cup milk
5 large egg yolks
2 large eggs
6 ounces semisweet chocolate, coarsely
chopped
2 teaspoons vanilla extract
3 medium bananas
1 tablespoon fresh lemon juice

Whipped cream, for garnish

YIELD: 8 to 10 servings

PREPARE THE CRUST: In a food processor, combine the flour, sugar, and salt and process briefly to combine. Add the butter and process until the mixture resembles coarse meal. With the machine running, add the egg yolk and ice water and process just until the dough masses together. Gather the dough into a ball, flatten into a large disk, and then press into a 9-inch pie plate; trim and crimp the edges. Freeze for 10 minutes.

Preheat the oven to 425°. Line the pie crust loosely with foil and fill with dried beans, rice or metal pie weights. Bake for 10 minutes. Reduce the oven temperature to 350°, remove the weights and bake for 10 minutes longer, or until golden brown. Set the crust on a wire rack to cool completely.

MAKE THE FILLING: In a saucepan, combine the sugar, cornstarch, salt, cream, and milk. Bring to a simmer over medium heat, stirring constantly to dissolve the sugar, about 12 minutes. Remove from the heat.

In a small bowl, beat the egg yolks and eggs. Whisk about ¼ cup of the cream mixture into the eggs to warm them. Transfer the warmed eggs to the saucepan. Cook over medium heat, stirring constantly, until the custard is of pudding consistency, about 6 minutes; do not boil. Remove from the heat, add the chocolate, and let stand for 1 minute. Add the vanilla and stir until the chocolate is melted.

Spread half of the custard in the cooled pie crust. Slice and arrange 1½ bananas over the custard. Top with the remaining custard. Slice the remaining 1½ bananas and toss the slices with the lemon juice; drain well. Arrange the banana slices over the custard. Cover the pie with plastic wrap and refrigerate until well chilled, about 4 hours.

Serve the pie garnished with rosettes of whipped cream.

# Puddings, Mousses
# & Soufflés

# Caramel and Chocolate Mousse Parfait

*2 cups heavy cream*
*¾ cup sugar*
*⅓ cup water*
*4 tablespoons (¼ cup) unsalted butter, softened*
*1 teaspoon vanilla extract*
*Chocolate Mousse (page 65)*

*Whipped cream, for garnish*

YIELD: *8 servings*

In a small saucepan, bring 1 cup of the cream to a simmer. Remove from the heat and set aside.

In a small heavy saucepan, dissolve the sugar in the water over low heat, stirring constantly. Bring to a boil over medium-high heat, then let boil without stirring until the syrup turns a deep amber. While the syrup is boiling, brush down the sides of the pan from time to time with a wet pastry brush to prevent crystals from forming. Remove the pan from the heat and stir in the hot cream (be careful, it will bubble rapidly) and the butter; stir until smooth. Transfer the caramel to a small bowl, cover, and refrigerate until cold, about 1½ hours.

In a medium bowl, beat the remaining 1 cup cream with the vanilla until soft peaks form. Gently fold in the chilled caramel and refrigerate.

Set out eight clear, stemmed glasses. Spoon a layer of Chocolate Mousse into each glass, using half of the mousse; smooth the surfaces. Top with layers of caramel mousse in each glass, using half of the mousse; smooth the surfaces. Repeat, spooning in second layers of both the Chocolate Mousse and the caramel mousse.

Top with rosettes of whipped cream.

# Chocolate Crème Brûlée

Preheat the oven to 300°. In a medium saucepan, bring the cream to a simmer. Remove the pan from the heat. Add the chocolate and stir until smooth and melted.

In a medium bowl, whisk the egg yolks. Beat in ¼ cup of the granulated sugar. Slowly whisk the hot chocolate mixture into the yolks. Whisk in the vanilla. Cool to room temperature.

Arrange six 6-ounce ramekins or custard cups in a baking pan. Divide the chocolate mixture among the ramekins. Fill the pan with water so it comes halfway up the sides of the cups. Bake for 40 minutes, or until the custard is set. Remove the custards from the water and cool on wire racks. Refrigerate the custards overnight.

Preheat the broiler. In a small bowl, thoroughly combine the remaining 2 tablespoons granulated sugar with the brown sugar. Toss to break up any clumps in the brown sugar. Sprinkle the sugar mixture evenly over the tops of the custards.

Broil the custards 2 inches from the heat source for 1 minute, or less, to melt the sugar. Watch the custards carefully so that the sugar melts and lightly caramelizes but does not burn. Let stand for 5 minutes before serving.

*2 cups heavy cream*
*3 ounces semisweet chocolate, finely chopped*
*6 large egg yolks*
*¼ cup plus 2 tablespoons granulated sugar*
*2 teaspoons vanilla extract*
*2 tablespoons dark brown sugar*

YIELD: *6 servings*

*For the water bath, choose a baking pan large enough for the ramekins to fit comfortably without touching one another. Pour hot water into the pan to come halfway up the sides of the ramekins.*

# Lemony Chocolate-Flecked Soufflés

### SOUFFLES
1 cup heavy cream
4 teaspoons finely grated lemon peel
½ cup sugar
1 tablespoon cornstarch
3 tablespoons fresh lemon juice
3 large egg yolks
1 tablespoon lemon jam or
marmalade (optional)
6 egg whites
¼ teaspoon cream of tartar
4 ounces semisweet chocolate, coarsely
chopped

### VANILLA CREAM
2 large egg yolks
½ cup sugar
1 cup heavy cream
½ teaspoon vanilla extract

YIELD: 6 servings

Preheat the oven to 375°. Butter and sugar six 10-ounce soufflé dishes or custard dishes and place them on a baking sheet.

MAKE THE SOUFFLES: In a small saucepan, bring the cream and lemon peel to a simmer. Remove from the heat, cover, and let steep for 15 minutes.

In a small bowl, whisk together ¼ cup of the sugar and the cornstarch. Whisk in the lemon juice and egg yolks until smooth.

Whisking constantly, add the hot cream to the egg yolk mixture. Strain the lemon cream mixture back into the saucepan and cook, stirring constantly, until thickened; do not boil. Transfer the lemon cream to a large bowl and set aside to cool for 15 minutes. Stir in the lemon jam, if using.

In a medium bowl with an electric mixer, beat the egg whites until foamy. Add the cream of tartar and beat until soft peaks form. Slowly beat in the remaining ¼ cup sugar and continue beating until stiff peaks form.

Fold one-third of the beaten whites into the cooled lemon cream to lighten it. Then fold in the remaining whites along with the chopped chocolate.

Divide the soufflé mixture among the prepared soufflé dishes. Place the baking sheet in the oven and bake for 18 to 20 minutes, or until puffed and golden brown on top.

MEANWHILE, MAKE THE VANILLA CREAM: In a small bowl, whisk the yolks and sugar together.

In a small saucepan, bring the cream to a simmer. Whisking constantly, beat the hot cream into the yolk mixture. Transfer this custard to the saucepan and cook over low heat, stirring constantly, until the custard coats the back of a spoon. Remove from the heat and stir in the vanilla.

Strain the vanilla cream into a sauceboat and serve alongside the soufflés.

# Chocolate Mousse Cups

In a small heavy saucepan, bring ½ cup of the heavy cream to a simmer. Remove from the heat, stir in the chocolate, and cover. Set aside for 5 minutes, then stir until smooth. Transfer the chocolate cream to a large bowl.

In another large bowl, with an electric mixer, beat the remaining 1½ cups cream with the sugar and vanilla until soft peaks form. Fold one-third of the whipped cream into the chocolate mixture to lighten it. Gently fold in the remaining whipped cream.

TO ASSEMBLE: Pipe the mousse decoratively into the Chocolate Dessert Cups (or simply spoon the mousse into individual dessert bowls). Garnish with candied violets, if desired.

*2 cups heavy cream*
*6 ounces semisweet chocolate, finely chopped*
*¼ cup confectioners' sugar*
*1 teaspoon vanilla extract*
*Chocolate Dessert Cups (page 102)*

*Candied violets, for garnish (optional)*

YIELD: *8 to 12 servings*

# White Chocolate Soufflé

### SOUFFLE
8 ounces white chocolate, coarsely
chopped
½ cup sugar
⅓ cup milk
4 large egg yolks
1 teaspoon vanilla extract
6 large egg whites
½ teaspoon cream of tartar

### RASPBERRY SAUCE
One 12-ounce package unsweetened
frozen raspberries
¼ cup sugar
1 tablespoon orange juice

Confectioners' sugar, for dusting

YIELD: *6 to 8 servings*

MAKE THE SOUFFLE: In a double boiler, melt the white chocolate over hot, not simmering, water. Set aside to cool slightly.

Preheat the oven to 350°. Butter and sugar a 2½-quart soufflé dish.

In a small saucepan, combine the sugar and milk. Cook over medium heat, stirring constantly, until the sugar dissolves, about 3 minutes. Transfer the mixture to a medium bowl. Whisk in the melted white chocolate, egg yolks, and vanilla until well blended.

In a medium bowl, beat the egg whites and cream of tartar until stiff peaks form. Fold the egg whites into the white chocolate mixture.

Spoon the mixture into the prepared soufflé dish. With a knife, cut a circle into the top of the soufflé 1 inch in from the edge and about 1 inch deep. Bake the soufflé for 25 to 30 minutes, or until the top is puffed, golden brown, and firm (the inside will still be jiggly).

MEANWHILE, MAKE THE SAUCE: Drain the berries in a fine-mesh sieve set over a bowl; press gently on the berries to remove as much juice as possible. Transfer the juice to a small saucepan and simmer until reduced to about ⅓ cup. Return the reduced juice to the bowl and stir in the sugar and orange juice. With a wooden spoon press the raspberries through the strainer into the bowl. Stir to combine the purée with the juice.

Remove the soufflé from the oven, dust with confectioners' sugar, and serve immediately with the raspberry sauce.

# The Really Easy Chocolate Dessert

In a medium saucepan, melt the chocolate with the cream, stirring constantly. Whisking constantly, stir in the beaten egg and cook, continuing to stir, until bubbles appear on the surface. Remove from the heat.

Pour the mixture into a blender, add the vanilla, and mix on high speed for 1 minute.

Pour the chocolate cream into dessert cups or glasses and chill until ready to serve. Serve garnished with banana slices, whipped cream, and chocolate sprinkles.

*7 ounces semisweet chocolate,*
*coarsely chopped*
*1 cup heavy cream*
*1 large egg, well beaten*
*2 teaspoons vanilla extract*

*Sliced bananas, whipped cream, and*
*chocolate sprinkles, for garnish*

YIELD: *4 servings*

*Pour the chocolate cream from the blender container directly into dessert cups or stemmed glasses.*

# Chocolate Soufflé with Caramel Crème Anglaise

*4 tablespoons (¼ cup) unsalted butter*
*3 tablespoons unsweetened cocoa powder*
*2 tablespoons cornstarch*
*½ cup milk*
*6 ounces semisweet chocolate, finely chopped*
*3 large egg yolks*
*2 teaspoons vanilla extract*
*6 large egg whites*
*½ teaspoon cream of tartar*
*½ cup sugar*

## CARAMEL CREME ANGLAISE
*¾ cup sugar*
*¼ cup water*
*1½ cups heavy cream, scalded*
*1 stick (½ cup) unsalted butter, softened*
*4 large egg yolks*
*1 teaspoon vanilla extract*

*Chocolate Scrolls (page 101) and confectioners' sugar, for garnish*

*YIELD: 6 servings*

Preheat the oven to 350°. Butter and sugar six 8-ounce soufflé dishes. Place the dishes on a baking sheet.

MAKE THE SOUFFLE: In a double boiler, melt the butter. Add the cocoa and cornstarch, and stir until smooth. Slowly stir in the milk until smooth. Add the chocolate and remove from the heat for 5 minutes; stir until smooth.

In a small bowl, stir together the yolks and vanilla. Whisk ½ cup of the chocolate mixture into the yolks to warm them. Whisk the warmed yolks into the chocolate mixture in the double boiler.

In a medium bowl, beat the egg whites until foamy. Add the cream of tartar and beat until soft peaks form. Slowly add the sugar and beat until stiff, glossy peaks form.

Transfer the chocolate mixture to a large bowl. Stir one-fourth of the egg whites into the mixture to lighten it. Gently but thoroughly fold in the remaining whites. Transfer the mixture to the soufflé dishes. Place the baking sheet on the bottom rack of the oven and bake for 25 to 30 minutes, or until a toothpick inserted halfway between the edge and the center comes out clean.

MEANWHILE, MAKE THE CREME ANGLAISE: In a heavy medium saucepan, dissolve the sugar in the water over low heat, stirring constantly. Bring to a boil over medium-high heat, then boil without stirring until the syrup turns a deep amber. While the syrup is boiling, brush down the sides of the pan occasionally to keep crystals from forming. Remove from the heat and stir in the cream (be careful, it will bubble rapidly) and butter; stir to dissolve the caramel.

In a small bowl, beat the egg yolks. Whisk ½ cup of the hot caramel into the yolks to warm them. Transfer the warmed yolks to the saucepan and stir over low heat until the sauce thickens and heavily coats the back of a spoon, about 5 minutes. Remove from the heat and stir in the vanilla. Strain the sauce through a sieve and keep warm. Garnish the soufflés with Chocolate Scrolls and confectioners' sugar. Serve with the caramel crème anglaise.

# White Chocolate Bread Pudding

Preheat the oven to 350°. Lightly butter a 9-by-13-inch baking dish.

Place the chocolate in a medium bowl. In a large heavy saucepan, bring the cream and granulated sugar to a simmer. Pour the hot cream over the chocolate. Let stand, covered, for 5 minutes, then stir until smooth. Beat the eggs and vanilla into the chocolate mixture.

Butter the bread slices and then cut into cubes. Layer half of the bread into the bottom of the prepared baking dish. Top the bread layer with the banana slices. Top with the remaining bread, then pour in the custard. Press the top of the pudding gently with a spatula to be sure that the bread at the top soaks up some of the custard. Cover the dish with aluminum foil.

Bake the pudding for 45 minutes, or until the custard is set.

Meanwhile, in a small bowl, combine the brown sugar and cinnamon.

When the pudding is set, remove the foil and sprinkle evenly with the cinnamon topping and return to the oven; increase the oven temperature to 450° and bake for 3 to 4 minutes to brown the top and caramelize the topping.

Cut into rectangles and serve warm, garnished with whipped cream and banana slices.

*16 ounces white chocolate, coarsely chopped*
*4 cups light cream or half-and-half*
*½ cup granulated sugar*
*8 large eggs, lightly beaten*
*1 tablespoon vanilla extract*
*6 tablespoons unsalted butter, softened*
*10 ounces day-old French bread, cut into ¾-inch-thick slices*
*2 bananas, sliced*
*2 tablespoons light brown sugar*
*2 teaspoons cinnamon*

*Whipped cream and banana slices, for garnish*

YIELD: *12 servings*

# Chocolate Caramel Custard

### CARAMEL
*1½ cups sugar*
*¼ cup water*

### CHOCOLATE CUSTARD
*8 egg yolks*
*½ cup sugar*
*2 cups light cream*
*6 ounces semisweet chocolate, finely chopped*
*1 teaspoon vanilla extract*

*Whipped cream and chocolate shavings, for garnish*

YIELD: *8 servings*

Preheat the oven to 325°.

MAKE THE CARAMEL: In a small heavy saucepan, dissolve the sugar in the water over low heat. Bring to a boil over medium-high heat, stirring constantly, then let boil without stirring until the syrup turns a deep amber. Quickly remove from the heat and pour an equal quantity of caramel syrup into each of eight 4-ounce ramekins. Place the ramekins in a large baking dish or roasting pan; set aside.

PREPARE THE CHOCOLATE CUSTARD: In a medium bowl, whisk together the egg yolks and sugar until smooth.

In a medium saucepan, bring the cream to a simmer. Gradually whisk the hot cream into the yolk-sugar mixture. Add the chocolate and vanilla and stir until smooth.

Strain the custard mixture through a sieve. Dividing evenly, pour the custard into the prepared ramekins. Pour hot water into the baking dish (or roasting pan) to come halfway up the sides of the ramekins. Bake the custards in the middle of the oven for about 30 minutes, or until they are set. Remove from the hot-water bath and set on wire racks to cool to room temperature.

Cover and refrigerate for at least 4 hours or overnight. Serve with a rosette of whipped cream and chocolate shavings.

# Mocha Soufflé

Preheat the oven to 350°. Butter six 6-ounce soufflé dishes.

In a medium saucepan, combine the milk and 1 cup of the sugar. Cook, stirring occasionally, over medium-low heat until the sugar dissolves, 5 to 10 minutes. Reduce the heat to low. Add the chocolate and coffee granules, then stir until the mixture is melted and smooth. Set aside to cool to lukewarm.

In a large bowl, beat the egg whites until foamy. Slowly add the remaining ¼ cup sugar and beat until stiff but not dry peaks form. In a medium bowl, lightly beat the egg yolks.

Whisk the chocolate mixture into the yolks until well blended. Whisk one-fourth of the egg whites into the chocolate mixture to lighten it. Gently and thoroughly fold in the remaining egg whites.

Divide the mixture evenly among the prepared soufflé dishes. Bake for 10 to 12 minutes, or until puffed. Remove from the oven, dust with confectioners' sugar, and serve immediately.

*½ cup milk*
*1¼ cups sugar*
*6 ounces unsweetened chocolate,*
*finely chopped*
*2 teaspoons instant espresso granules*
*6 large egg whites*
*4 large egg yolks*

*Confectioners' sugar, for dusting*

YIELD: *8 servings*

*With a whisk, beat one-fourth of the egg whites into the chocolate mixture to lighten it (far left). Then, with a spatula, gently but thoroughly fold in the remaining egg whites (near left), taking care not to deflate the soufflé mixture.*

# Mocha Pudding Cake

❖

## CAKE

*1 ounce unsweetened chocolate, finely chopped*
*1 tablespoon unsalted butter*
*1 cup all-purpose flour*
*⅔ cup granulated sugar*
*1 teaspoon instant espresso granules*
*½ teaspoon baking powder*
*½ teaspoon baking soda*
*¼ teaspoon salt*
*½ cup milk*

## SAUCE

*⅔ cup (packed) light brown sugar*
*4 tablespoons (¼ cup) unsalted butter*
*2 ounces unsweetened chocolate, finely chopped*
*⅛ teaspoon salt*
*1 cup very hot, freshly brewed coffee*
*1 tablespoon coffee liqueur*

*Coffee ice cream, for serving*

YIELD: *6 servings*

Preheat the oven to 350°. Lightly butter six 6-ounce custard cups.

MAKE THE CAKES: In a double boiler, melt the chocolate and the butter. Set aside to cool slightly.

In a medium bowl, combine the flour, granulated sugar, espresso granules, baking powder, baking soda, and salt. Gradually blend in the melted chocolate mixture and the milk. Dividing evenly, pour the batter into the prepared custard cups.

FOR THE SAUCE: Place the brown sugar, butter, chocolate, and salt in a medium bowl. Pour the hot coffee over the chocolate mixture and let stand for 1 minute. Add the coffee liqueur and whisk until the chocolate and butter are melted and the mixture is smooth.

Dividing evenly, spoon the pudding sauce over the cake batter; do not stir. Bake for 30 minutes, or until the cakes are just firm to the touch. (The bottom of the cakes, where the sauce ends up, will stay very liquid.)

Let the cakes stand for 10 to 15 minutes. Invert the cakes onto dessert plates, making sure to get all of the sauce. Serve warm with a scoop of coffee ice cream.

*Spoon the pudding sauce on top of the cake batter in the custard cups. Do not stir. The sauce will sink to the bottom of the cups as the pudding cakes bake.*

# White Chocolate Cream with Apricots

Preheat the oven to 325°.

In a small bowl, combine the apricots and apricot brandy and set aside.

In a medium bowl, whisk the egg yolks and sugar. In a medium saucepan, bring the cream to a simmer over medium heat. Remove the pan from the heat. Add the white chocolate and stir until melted and smooth, about 5 minutes. Slowly whisk the warm white chocolate mixture into the egg yolks. Whisk in the vanilla.

Measure out 2 teaspoons of the brandy that the apricots are soaking in and stir it into the custard. Set aside the remaining apricots until serving time.

Arrange six 4-ounce ramekins or custard cups in a roasting pan. Spoon the custard into the cups. Fill the pan with enough hot water to come halfway up the sides of the cups. Bake for 35 minutes, or until the custard is set. Remove the custards from the water and cool on wire racks. Refrigerate until thoroughly chilled, about 4 hours.

In a double boiler, melt the semisweet chocolate with the oil over hot, not simmering, water. Set aside to cool slightly. Drain the apricots and discard the brandy.

Spoon the warm chocolate into a pastry bag fitted with a very small round tip. Top the chilled custards with the drained, diced apricots and pipe the apricots with the chocolate.

*¼ cup diced dried apricots*
*¼ cup apricot brandy*
*5 large egg yolks*
*¼ cup sugar*
*2 cups heavy cream*
*5 ounces white chocolate, finely chopped*
*½ teaspoon vanilla extract*
*2 ounces semisweet chocolate, finely chopped*
*½ teaspoon vegetable oil*

YIELD: *6 servings*

# *Double-Chocolate Trifle*

*2 cups heavy cream*
*10 ounces semisweet chocolate, finely chopped*
*3 tablespoons sugar*
*Pinch of salt*
*4 large egg yolks*
*1 teaspoon vanilla extract*
*1 pound of chocolate pound cake, cut into ¼-inch-thick slices*
*⅓ cup coffee liqueur*
*1 pint strawberries, cut into thin slices*

*Whipped cream and unsweetened cocoa powder, for garnish*

Yield: *8 to 10 servings*

In a double boiler, heat the cream with the chocolate, sugar, and salt, stirring frequently, until the mixture is melted and smooth.

In a medium bowl, lightly beat the egg yolks. Whisk about one-fourth of the chocolate cream into the yolks to warm them. Transfer the warmed yolks to the chocolate cream in the double boiler and cook over simmering water, stirring frequently, until the custard just begins to thicken.

Pour the custard into a large bowl and stir in the vanilla. Place a piece of plastic wrap directly on the filling to prevent a skin from forming and set aside.

Stack the cake slices and cut them into quarters (there should be about 5 cups). Place half of the cake slices in the bottom of a 2-quart, straight-sided, flat-bottomed bowl (preferably glass). Sprinkle the cake with half of the coffee liqueur. Top with half of the chocolate custard and half of the sliced strawberries. Repeat the layering.

Cover and chill for 2 to 3 hours. Just before serving, pipe rosettes of whipped cream over the trifle. Dust with cocoa powder.

# Ice Cream & Frozen Desserts

# Decadent White Chocolate Ice Cream

18 ounces white chocolate, coarsely
chopped
2 cups half-and-half or light cream
6 large egg yolks
¾ cup sugar
1¼ cups heavy cream, chilled
2 teaspoons vanilla extract

Pieces of cookie, for garnish

YIELD: *About 5 cups*

In a double boiler, melt 14 ounces of the chocolate over hot, not simmering, water. Set aside to cool slightly.

In a medium saucepan, bring the half-and-half just to a simmer over medium heat. Remove the pan from the heat.

In a double boiler, whisk together the egg yolks and sugar until pale. Slowly whisk in the hot half-and-half until well blended. Cook over simmering water, whisking constantly, until thick enough to coat the back of a spoon, about 12 minutes. Remove the double boiler top from the water.

Add the melted chocolate, stirring until well blended. Stir in the chilled heavy cream and the vanilla. Refrigerate the ice cream mixture until well chilled, at least 4 hours.

Stir the reserved 4 ounces of chopped white chocolate into the mixture and transfer to an ice cream maker. Freeze according to the manufacturer's directions. Serve the ice cream soft-frozen or transfer to an airtight container and freeze until serving time. Garnish each serving with pieces of cookie, if desired.

# Super Hot Fudge Sauce

In a heavy medium saucepan, combine the chocolate, butter, cocoa, sugar, water, and corn syrup. Whisk over medium-high heat until the chocolate and butter are melted and the sugar is dissolved. When the sauce just comes to a boil, reduce the heat to low and cook at a low boil for 8 to 10 minutes; the sauce will thicken as it cools. (If the sauce is too thick, thin it with a little water.) Add the vanilla and stir to combine. Store in the refrigerator tightly covered.

*4 ounces semisweet chocolate, coarsely chopped*
*5 tablespoons unsalted butter*
*¼ cup unsweetened cocoa powder*
*¾ cup sugar*
*¾ cup water*
*¼ cup light corn syrup*
*2 teaspoons vanilla extract*

YIELD: *About 1½ cups*

# Chocolate Chunk Ice Cream Sandwiches

2½ cups all-purpose flour
½ teaspoon baking soda
¼ teaspoon salt
1 cup granulated sugar
½ cup (packed) light brown sugar
2 sticks (1 cup) unsalted butter
2 large eggs
1 teaspoon vanilla extract
8 ounces semisweet chocolate, cut into chunks
2 cups mini semisweet chocolate chips
2 quarts chocolate ice cream, slightly softened

YIELD: *16 ice cream sandwiches*

*When rolling the ice cream sandwiches in the chocolate chips, press lightly to even out the edges of the ice cream.*

Preheat the oven to 300°. In a medium bowl, whisk together the flour, baking soda, and salt.

In a large bowl with an electric mixer, blend the granulated and brown sugars. Add the butter and beat to form a grainy paste. Add the eggs, one at a time, and the vanilla, then beat at medium speed until fully combined. Add the flour mixture and blend at low speed until just combined; do not over-mix. Fold in the chocolate chunks.

For each cookie, drop 2 tablespoons of dough onto an ungreased cookie sheet, leaving about 3 inches space between the cookies. Pat the dough lightly to a ¼-inch thickness.

Bake for 20 to 22 minutes, or until the cookies are lightly browned around the edges. Cool for 5 minutes on the cookie sheet, then transfer the cookies to a wire rack to cool completely.

Place the chocolate chips in a shallow bowl or plate. Spread ½ cup of ice cream on each of 16 cookies. Top with a second cookie and press the two halves together to push the ice cream slightly beyond the edges of the cookies. Roll the edges of the ice cream sandwiches in the chocolate chips to coat them and to even out the edges of the sandwich. Wrap each sandwich tightly in plastic wrap and freeze until firm, about 4 hours.

# Chocolate Caramel Ice Cream

In medium bowl, whisk the yolks and salt until combined.

In heavy medium saucepan, dissolve the sugar in the water over low heat. Bring to a boil over medium-high heat, stirring constantly, then boil without stirring until the syrup turns a deep amber. Remove the pan from the heat and carefully stir in the half-and-half (be careful, the mixture will bubble rapidly). Return to the heat and continue cooking, stirring to dissolve any hardened caramel. Cook until the mixture comes to a gentle boil, 7 to 10 minutes.

Whisk about half of the hot caramel mixture into the egg yolks to warm them. Return the warmed eggs to the saucepan and continue cooking over low heat, stirring constantly, until the mixture coats the back of a spoon, about 10 minutes. Whisk in the chocolate until smooth.

Strain the ice cream base into a bowl and let cool to room temperature. Refrigerate until well chilled, at least 4 hours or overnight.

Transfer the mixture to an ice cream maker and freeze according to the manufacturer's directions. Serve the ice cream soft-frozen, or transfer to an air-tight container and freeze until serving time.

*4 large egg yolks*
*⅛ teaspoon salt*
*¾ cup sugar*
*2 tablespoons water*
*3 cups half-and-half or light cream,*
*at room temperature*
*4 ounces semisweet or bittersweet*
*chocolate, finely chopped*

YIELD: *1½ pints*

2 bananas
2 cups coarsely chopped milk
chocolate
1 cup finely chopped macadamia
nuts

YIELD: *4 servings*

Cut the bananas in half crosswise. Insert a popsicle stick into the cut end of each banana half. Wrap each banana popsicle in foil and place in the freezer until frozen.

In a double boiler, melt the chocolate over hot, not simmering, water. Stir until smooth. Remove from the heat.

Place the chopped nuts on a sheet of wax paper. Dip the frozen bananas into the melted chocolate and, just as the chocolate is beginning to set but is still slightly soft, roll the bananas in the nuts.

Serve immediately or rewrap in foil and return to the freezer.

*The safest method of melting chocolate is in a double boiler; the modified heat keeps the chocolate from scorching. Just be sure that the chocolate is melted over hot and not simmering water: If the steam released by boiling or simmering water condenses in the chocolate, it will cause the melted chocolate to stiffen or "seize."*

# *Creamy Mocha Ice Cream Shake*

MAKE THE FUDGE SAUCE: In a heavy medium saucepan, combine the chocolate, butter, cocoa, sugar, water, and corn syrup. Whisk over medium-high heat until the chocolate and butter are melted and the sugar is dissolved. When the sauce just comes to a boil, reduce the heat to low and cook at a low boil for 8 to 10 minutes; the sauce will thicken as it cools. Add the vanilla and stir to combine. Let cool to room temperature, then store in the refrigerator until ready to use. (This fudge sauce recipe makes enough for six ice cream shakes. If you are only making two, refrigerate the remaining fudge sauce and keep on hand as an ice cream topping.)

MAKE THE SHAKES: In a blender, combine ½ cup of the fudge sauce, the milk, coffee granules, and coffee liqueur (if using). Process until smooth. Add the ice cream and blend until smooth and thick.

Pour the shakes into tall glasses and garnish with whipped cream rosettes and chocolate shavings.

### FUDGE SAUCE
*4 ounces semisweet chocolate, coarsely chopped*
*5 tablespoons unsalted butter*
*¼ cup unsweetened cocoa powder*
*¾ cup sugar*
*¾ cup water*
*¼ cup light corn syrup*
*2 teaspoons vanilla extract*

### SHAKES
*½ cup milk*
*1 teaspoon instant coffee granules*
*1 teaspoon coffee liqueur (optional)*
*1½ cups vanilla ice cream*

*Whipped cream and chocolate shavings, for garnish*

YIELD: *2 servings*

# Sweetie Pie Cookie Dough Ice Cream

2 ounces unsweetened chocolate
1 ¾ cups semisweet chocolate chips
1 stick (½ cup) unsalted butter
1 cup sugar
2 teaspoons vanilla extract
2 tablespoons water
1 cup all-purpose flour
½ cup white chocolate chips
¼ cup milk chocolate chips
2 quarts chocolate or vanilla ice cream, slightly softened

*Super Hot Fudge Sauce (page 79) and mixed chocolate chips, for garnish*

YIELD: *About 3 quarts*

In a double boiler, melt the unsweetened chocolate and ¾ cup of the chocolate chips over hot, not simmering, water. Stir until smooth.

In a medium bowl, cream the butter and sugar. Add the vanilla and water and beat until smooth. Beat in the melted chocolate. Add the flour, white chocolate chips, milk chocolate chips, and remaining 1 cup semisweet chocolate chips; mix at low speed until the chips are evenly distributed throughout the dough.

Drop the dough by the teaspoon into the softened ice cream and stir to mix, partially blending the dough into the ice cream. Return to the freezer to firm up before serving.

If desired, serve the ice cream with Super Hot Fudge Sauce and a sprinkling of chocolate chips.

*Drop the cookie dough by the teaspoon into the softened ice cream and stir to incorporate, being careful to leave streaks of cookie dough throughout.*

In a double boiler, melt the chocolate over hot, not simmering, water. Set aside to cool slightly.

Meanwhile, beat the egg whites with a pinch of cream of tartar until stiff peaks form.

In a small saucepan, boil the sugar and water with another pinch of cream of tartar until it reaches 234° to 240° on a candy thermometer (soft-ball stage), 10 to 12 minutes.

With the mixer going, carefully pour the hot sugar syrup into the egg whites to make a stiff, glossy meringue. Fold the melted chocolate into the meringue to make chewy lumps.

In a medium bowl, beat the heavy cream until soft peaks form. Add the crème de menthe and keep beating until stiff peaks form. Fold the chopped chocolate chips into the whipped cream, then fold the whipped cream into the chocolate meringue, leaving streaks of whipped cream. Spoon the mousse into individual dessert bowls or glasses, cover with plastic wrap and freeze until firm, about 2 hours.

Serve garnished with whipped cream and fresh mint.

*8 ounces semisweet chocolate, finely chopped*
*2 large egg whites*
*2 pinches of cream of tartar*
*½ cup sugar*
*¼ cup water*
*1 cup heavy cream, chilled*
*3 tablespoons crème de menthe*
*⅓ cup semisweet chocolate chips, coarsely chopped*

*Whipped cream and fresh mint, for garnish*

YIELD: *4 to 6 servings*

# Ice Cream Brownie Sandwich

## BROWNIES

6 ounces semisweet chocolate, coarsely
chopped
1 stick (½ cup) unsalted butter
2 cups all-purpose flour
1 teaspoon baking soda
½ teaspoon salt
1½ cups (packed) light brown sugar
4 large eggs
6 ounces mini semisweet chocolate
chips

## ASSEMBLY AND GLAZE

3 cups ice cream, softened slightly
½ cup heavy cream
6 ounces semisweet chocolate chips

White chocolate hearts,
for garnish

YIELD: 32 ice cream sandwiches

Preheat the oven to 350°. Butter the bottom of an 11-by-17-inch jelly-roll pan. Line the pan with parchment or wax paper and butter the paper.

MAKE THE BROWNIES: In a double boiler, melt the chocolate and butter over hot, not simmering, water, stirring until melted. Set aside to cool to room temperature.

In a small bowl, whisk together the flour, baking soda, and salt.

In a medium bowl, beat the sugar and eggs together until thickened, about 5 minutes. Beat in the melted chocolate mixture. Fold in the flour mixture and the mini chocolate chips. Pour the batter into the prepared pan and smooth the surface. Bake for 15 minutes, or until a cake tester comes out clean. Cool the cake in the pan on a rack for 10 minutes.

Carefully invert the cake onto a work surface and peel off the parchment paper. With a 2-inch round cookie cutter, cut cookies out from the brownie while it is still slightly warm. Place the brownie rounds in the freezer while you soften up the ice cream in the refrigerator for 20 minutes.

ASSEMBLE THE SANDWICHES: Cut each brownie round horizontally in half. Spread one half with ¼ inch (about 4 teaspoons) of softened ice cream and top with the other half. As you work, place each finished sandwich in the freezer so it does not melt as you assemble the remaining sandwiches. Freeze the sandwiches until firm.

MEANWHILE, MAKE THE GLAZE: In a small heavy saucepan, scald the cream. Remove from the heat, add the chocolate chips, cover, and let sit for 5 minutes. Stir until smooth. Keep warm and pourable.

Set the ice cream sandwiches on a wire rack set over a baking sheet. Spoon the warm glaze over the top of the sandwich letting it run down the sides to cover the sandwich completely. Repeat with the remaining sandwiches. Garnish each sandwich with a white chocolate heart, if desired. Return to the freezer to set the glaze and firm the ice cream, about 30 minutes.

# Candy &
# Decorations

❖

# White Fudge with Almonds

1 cup slivered almonds
¾ cup sugar
⅔ cup evaporated milk
½ cup marshmallow creme
2 tablespoons unsalted butter
¼ teaspoon salt
10 ounces white chocolate, finely chopped
¼ teaspoon almond extract

YIELD: *About 1½ pounds*

Preheat the oven to 350°. Spread the almonds on a baking sheet and toast in the oven for 10 minutes or until golden. Cool the almonds slightly, then finely chop. Set aside.

Line an 8-inch square pan with foil so that the foil extends 2 inches beyond the pan on two opposite sides.

In a heavy medium saucepan, combine the sugar, evaporated milk, marshmallow creme, butter and salt. Bring to a boil over medium heat, stirring constantly, until the sugar and marshmallow creme dissolve, about 3 minutes.

Reduce the heat to low, cover, and simmer for 1 minute; do not stir. Uncover the pan and cook for 5 minutes, stirring frequently. Remove the pan from the heat and add the white chocolate; stir until melted and smooth. Stir in the nuts and almond extract.

Scrape the fudge into the prepared pan and smooth the top. Chill for 1 hour, or until firm. Remove the fudge from the pan by lifting up the edges of the foil. Cut the fudge into small squares.

Line a cookie sheet with aluminum foil.

In a double boiler, melt the semisweet and milk chocolates with the oil over hot, not simmering, water, stirring constantly until the chocolate is melted and smooth.

Remove the top part of the double boiler and let the chocolate cool to tepid. (The chocolate may thicken slightly as it cools.)

Stir the pecans and chopped white chocolate into the cooled melted chocolate and pour the mixture out onto the prepared cookie sheet. Spread to the desired thickness. Refrigerate for 20 to 30 minutes, or until set.

Slide a metal spatula under the chocolate to loosen from the foil. Break into uneven pieces.

*6 ounces semisweet chocolate, finely chopped*
*6 ounces milk chocolate, finely chopped*
*1 tablespoon vegetable oil*
*1 cup pecan halves and pieces, toasted*
*6 ounces white chocolate, coarsely chopped*

**YIELD:** *About 1¼ pounds*

# Nutty Milk Chocolate Fudge

1½ sticks (¾ cup) unsalted butter
⅓ cup evaporated milk
¼ cup sugar
6 ounces milk chocolate, finely
chopped
6 ounces semisweet chocolate, finely
chopped
1 cup marshmallow creme
1 cup peanut butter chips
½ cup unsalted, roasted peanuts,
coarsely chopped

YIELD: *About 2 pounds*

Line an 8-inch square pan with foil. Lightly butter the foil.

In a heavy medium saucepan, combine the butter, evaporated milk, and sugar. Bring the mixture to a boil, stirring constantly to dissolve the sugar. Reduce the heat and boil gently, without stirring, for 5 minutes.

Remove from the heat and stir in the milk chocolate, semisweet chocolate, and marshmallow creme; whisk until smooth. Set aside to cool to lukewarm.

Stir in the peanut butter chips and peanuts. Pour the mixture into the prepared pan and refrigerate until set, 3 to 4 hours. Cut the fudge into squares.

# *White Chocolate Pecan Sheets*

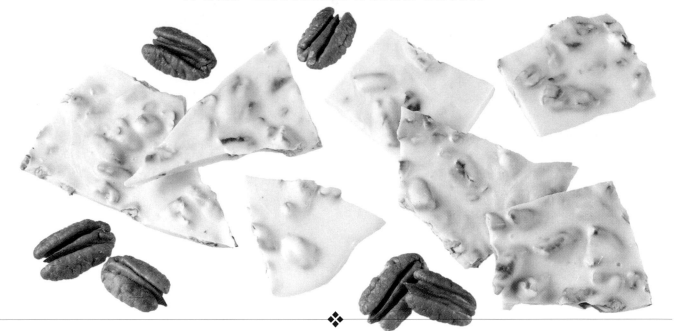

Line a baking sheet with aluminum foil.

In a double boiler, melt the chocolate with the butter and oil over hot, not simmering, water, stirring constantly until the chocolate is melted and smooth.

Remove the top part of the double boiler and stir the nuts into the melted chocolate. Pour the chocolate mixture out onto the prepared cookie sheet. Spread randomly to the desired thickness. Refrigerate for 20 to 30 minutes, or until set.

Slide a metal spatula under the chocolate to loosen from the foil. Break into uneven pieces. Store in an airtight container in the refrigerator.

*1 pound white chocolate, finely chopped*
*1 tablespoon unsalted butter*
*1 tablespoon vegetable oil*
*1 cup coarsely chopped toasted pecans or pistachios*

YIELD: *About 1¼ pounds*

*Spread the white chocolate mixture to an uneven thickness over the foil-lined baking sheet.*

6 ounces semisweet chocolate, finely
chopped
6 ounces milk chocolate, finely
chopped
1 tablespoon unsalted butter
1 tablespoon vegetable oil
1 cup chopped toasted almonds or
macadamia nuts
1 cup crisp rice cereal
6 ounces white chocolate, coarsely
chopped

YIELD: *About 1¼ pounds*

Line a cookie sheet with aluminum foil.

In a double boiler, melt the semisweet and milk chocolates with the butter and oil over hot, not simmering, water, stirring constantly until the chocolate is melted and smooth.

Remove the top part of the double boiler and let the chocolate cool to tepid. (The chocolate may thicken slightly as it cools.)

Stir the nuts, cereal, and white chocolate pieces into the cooled melted chocolate and pour the mixture out onto the prepared cookie sheet. Spread to the desired thickness. Refrigerate for 20 to 30 minutes, or until set.

Slide a metal spatula under the chocolate to loosen from the foil. Break into uneven pieces.

# Chocolate Peanut Butter Pieces

Line a 9-by-13-inch pan with foil.

In a double boiler, melt the chocolate over hot, not simmering, water. Stir until smooth.

Place the peanut butter in a small bowl. Gradually beat in the sugar.

Add the peanut butter mixture to the chocolate and stir until blended. Set aside to cool slightly.

Stir in ¾ cup of the peanuts and spread the mixture in the foil-lined pan. Smooth the top, then sprinkle the remaining ¼ cup peanuts over the top, pressing lightly into the candy. Chill until firm, then cut into pieces.

18 ounces milk chocolate, finely chopped (about 3 cups)
½ cup creamy peanut butter
5 tablespoons confectioners' sugar, sifted
1 cup salted peanuts, whole and halves

YIELD: *About 2 pounds*

*Use a wooden spoon to stir the peanut butter mixture into the melted chocolate.*

# E.G. Fudge

*1 cup (2 sticks) unsalted butter*
*3 cups sugar*
*½ cup unsweetened cocoa powder*
*Pinch of salt*
*3 tablespoons light corn syrup*
*1 cup condensed milk*
*½ cup water*
*1 teaspoon vanilla extract*
*1 cup coarsely chopped walnuts*
*2½ cups miniature marshmallows*

YIELD: *About 1½ pounds*

Butter an 8-inch square pan or 9-inch-diameter plate. Set aside the butter in a medium bowl.

In a large heavy saucepan, whisk together the sugar, cocoa, and salt. Add the corn syrup, condensed milk, and water, then stir with a wooden spoon until thoroughly combined. Cook over low-to-medium heat, stirring constantly, until the mixture comes to a full rolling boil. Boil, without stirring, until the mixture measures 236° (soft-ball stage) on a candy thermometer. To test for doneness, drop a teaspoon of the mixture in a bowl of iced water and form it into a ball with your fingers. If the ball holds its shape under water but immediately loses shape and flattens between your fingers out of the water, the mixture is ready; otherwise cook a little longer.

Remove from the heat and pour the chocolate mixture over the butter; do not stir. Let the mixture cool to lukewarm; you should be able to comfortably touch the sides of the bowl with your hands.

Beat at low speed with an electric mixer to incorporate the butter, then continue beating until the shine begins to come off the mixture (at this point you should be able to comfortably dip your finger in the mixture). Add the vanilla and beat for another 15 minutes or so, until the fudge starts to thicken and falls slowly from the beaters. Stir in the walnuts and marshmallows, then immediately spread the fudge in the prepared pan.

Let the fudge sit at room temperature until firm enough to cut, about 1 hour.

9

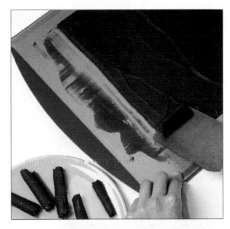

***For Chocolate Scrolls:***
*Use a metal spatula to spread melted chocolate on a cookie sheet or smooth work surface. Let the chocolate stand at room temperature until firmed up but still pliable. Use a wide spatula to scrape the chocolate into a roll. For a looser scroll, scrape up a shorter length of chocolate so that it does not completely close.*

***For Chocolate Cut-Outs:***
*Spread melted chocolate on a sheet of parchment paper or wax paper with a metal spatula. Let the chocolate stand at room temperature until firmed up but still pliable. Use small cookie cutters to cut out a variety of shapes. For more delicate shapes, use extra-small cutters often sold as truffle cutters or aspic cutters.*

***For Chocolate Dessert Cups:***
*With a small pastry brush, coat the insides of paper muffin-cup liners with melted chocolate. Chill the cups to set the chocolate and then brush on a second coat. If desired, for a sturdier cup, add a third coat. When the final coating is set, carefully peel off the paper.*

***For Chocolate Leaves:***
*With a small pastry brush, paint the underside (vein side) of a nontoxic leaf—the leaves shown here are lemon leaves—with melted chocolate; do not paint all the way to the edge of the leaf. Place the coated leaves in the refrigerator to set the chocolate, then very carefully peel the leaf away.*

# Showstoppers

❖

# Chocolate Pudding Soufflé Cake

## CAKE
*4 tablespoons (¼ cup) unsalted
butter
3 ounces unsweetened chocolate
½ cup cake flour
½ teaspoon baking powder
¼ teaspoon salt
6 large eggs—3 separated, 3 whole
1 cup sugar
¼ teaspoon cream of tartar*

## PUDDING
*5 large egg yolks
½ cup sugar
2 tablespoons cornstarch
2½ cups heavy cream
8 ounces semisweet chocolate, finely
chopped
2 teaspoons vanilla extract*

YIELD: *One 9-inch layer cake*

Preheat the oven to 375°. Butter a 9-inch springform pan.

MAKE THE CAKE: In a double boiler, melt the butter and unsweetened chocolate. Stir until smooth, then set aside. In a small bowl, whisk together the flour, baking powder, and salt. In a large bowl with an electric mixer, beat the 3 whole eggs and 3 egg yolks with ¾ cup of the sugar until pale and lemon-colored. Slowly beat in the chocolate mixture. Then beat in the flour mixture.

In a medium bowl, beat the egg whites until foamy. Add the cream of tartar and beat until soft peaks form. Beat in the remaining ¼ cup sugar until stiff glossy peaks form. Stir one-third of the egg whites into the batter to lighten it. Gently and thoroughly fold in the remaining whites. Transfer the batter to the prepared pan and smooth the top.

Bake for 40 to 50 minutes, or until the center is set. Transfer to a wire rack to cool to room temperature. Refrigerate until firm.

MEANWHILE, MAKE THE PUDDING: In a medium bowl, lightly beat the egg yolks. In a heavy medium saucepan, whisk together the sugar and cornstarch. Gradually whisk in the cream. Bring the mixture to a boil over low heat, whisking constantly.

Very gradually whisk the hot cream into the egg yolks, then return the mixture to the saucepan and cook over very low heat, whisking constantly, until the pudding is very thick and steamy; do not let it boil. Remove the pudding from the heat, stir in the chocolate and vanilla, and stir until melted and smooth. Transfer the pudding to a bowl, place a piece of plastic wrap directly on the surface, and refrigerate until cold, at least 2 hours.

TO ASSEMBLE: Remove the sides of the springform. With a long serrated knife, cut the cake horizontally into 3 even layers. Place one layer on a serving plate. Spread about ¾ cup of pudding on top. Top with a second layer and spread with another ¾ cup of pudding. Top with the third layer and spread the tops and sides with the remaining pudding. Refrigerate until set.

# The Ultimate Ice Cream Pie

Preheat the oven to 325°.

MAKE THE CRUST: Press the cookie crumbs into the bottom and up the sides of a 9-inch pie plate. Bake for 10 minutes. Cool to room temperature.

PREPARE THE FUDGE SAUCE: In a small saucepan, melt the chocolate and butter over low heat; stir until smooth. Add the sugar, cocoa, corn syrup, and water and cook until the sugar dissolves. Bring the mixture to a boil and cook at a low boil, without stirring, until the sauce is thick and smooth, about 15 minutes. Remove from the heat and stir in the vanilla. Set aside to cool to lukewarm.

MAKE THE CARAMEL SAUCE: In a heavy medium saucepan, dissolve the sugar in the water over low heat, stirring constantly. Bring to a boil over medium-high heat, then let boil, without stirring, until the syrup turns a light amber. While the syrup is boiling, brush down the sides of the pan from time to time with a wet pastry brush to prevent crystals from forming. Remove the pan from the heat and stir in the hot cream (it will bubble rapidly). Stir in the butter and continue stirring the sauce until smooth. Cool the sauce to lukewarm.

TO ASSEMBLE: Pour the fudge sauce into the pie crust. Chill in the freezer until the sauce is set, about 15 minutes. In a medium bowl, stir the marshmallows and chocolate chips into the softened ice cream. Spread the ice cream mixture over the fudge layer and smooth the top. Place in the freezer until set, about 30 minutes.

Dip a fork into the caramel sauce and drizzle it in a criss-cross pattern over the top of the pie. Return to the freezer for 1 hour to set. Cut the pie into wedges with a sharp knife and serve immediately.

COOKIE CRUMB CRUST
1¼ cups chocolate chip cookie crumbs

FUDGE SAUCE
2 ounces semisweet chocolate, chopped
2½ tablespoons unsalted butter
¼ cup plus 2 tablespoons sugar
2 tablespoons unsweetened cocoa powder
2 tablespoons corn syrup
¼ cup plus 2 tablespoons water
1 teaspoon vanilla extract

CARAMEL SAUCE
½ cup sugar
2 tablespoons water
¼ cup cream, scalded
2 tablespoons unsalted butter, softened

FILLING
1 cup miniature marshmallows
1 cup semisweet chocolate chips
3 cups vanilla ice cream, softened in the refrigerator

YIELD: *One 9-inch pie*

## CHOCOLATE MOUSSE
*3 ounces semisweet chocolate*
*¼ cup light corn syrup*
*¼ cup plus 2 tablespoons sugar*
*3 large egg yolks*
*1 teaspoon vanilla extract*
*1¼ cups heavy cream*

## ASSEMBLY
*2 quarts chocolate chip ice cream,*
*softened slightly*
*1¾ cups chocolate chip cookie crumbs*
*2 tablespoons unsalted butter,*
*softened*
*1 teaspoon unflavored gelatin*
*4 teaspoons water*
*2 cups heavy cream*
*¼ cup sugar*
*2 teaspoons vanilla extract*

YIELD: *6 to 8 servings*

Line a 2-quart, 9-inch-diameter stainless steel bowl with foil and place in the freezer while you make the mousse.

MAKE THE MOUSSE: In a double boiler, melt the chocolate over hot, not simmering, water. Set aside to cool to room temperature.

In a medium bowl set over a saucepan of simmering water, combine the corn syrup, sugar, and egg yolks. With an electric mixer, beat the egg yolk mixture constantly until it is very thick and pale and warm to the touch. Remove the bowl from the water bath and continue beating until the eggs are cool. Stir in the melted chocolate and vanilla.

In another medium bowl, beat the cream until soft peaks form. Stir one-fourth of the whipped cream into the chocolate mixture to lighten it, then gently but thoroughly fold in the remaining whipped cream. Chill the mousse in the freezer for 1 hour.

MEANWHILE, BEGIN TO ASSEMBLE THE BOMBE: Spread the softened ice cream in the chilled foil-lined bowl to a uniform thickness of about 1½ inches, extending up to the rim. Return to the freezer until firm.

Spoon the chilled mousse into the ice cream-lined bowl and smooth the surface. Return to the freezer for 1 hour.

Meanwhile, in a food processor or blender, combine the cookie crumbs and butter, then process until finely ground.

Press the cookie crumbs over the surface of the mousse and return to the freezer while you make the topping.

In a small heatproof measuring cup, combine the gelatin and water and set aside to soften, about 5 minutes. Place the measuring cup in a pan of simmering water and stir occasionally to dissolve the gelatin. Remove the cup and set aside to cool to room temperature.

In a medium bowl with an electric mixer, beat the cream with the sugar and vanilla until it is just beginning to thicken. Slowly pour in the cooled gelatin mixture, beating constantly. Beat the cream until stiff peaks form, being very careful not to overbeat. Immediately transfer the stabilized whipped cream to a pastry bag fitted with a medium (#5) star tip.

Remove the bombe from the freezer and invert onto a serving plate. Carefully remove the foil. Pipe rosettes of whipped cream over the surface of the bombe, starting at the base and working to the top. Serve immediately or return the bombe to the freezer until serving time.

*Spread the softened ice cream in the foil-lined bowl to a uniform thickness of 1½ inches.*

*Far left, fill the center of the bombe with the chilled chocolate mousse. Near left, decorate the surface of the unmolded bombe with rosettes of stabilized whipped cream.*

# Lemon Custard Cake

### CAKE

1½ cups cake flour
1 cup sugar
¾ teaspoon baking powder
½ teaspoon salt
1½ sticks (¾ cup) unsalted butter, softened
¼ cup sour cream
2 large eggs, at room temperature
¼ cup lemon juice
2 teaspoons grated lemon zest
½ teaspoon lemon extract

### VANILLA CUSTARD

1 cup heavy cream
1 large egg
2 large egg yolks
⅓ cup sugar
1 tablespoon plus 2 teaspoons cornstarch
1 teaspoon vanilla extract

### CHOCOLATE GANACHE

6 ounces semisweet chocolate, finely chopped
¾ cup heavy cream
2 tablespoons unsalted butter
2 tablespoons sugar

YIELD: *One 9-inch layer cake*

Preheat the oven to 350°. Butter a 9-inch cake pan, line the bottom with a circle of wax paper, then butter and flour the paper.

MAKE THE CAKE: In a large bowl, mix the flour, sugar, baking powder, and salt. Add the butter, sour cream, and 1 of the eggs. Mix until just blended. Add the remaining egg, the lemon juice, zest, and extract. Beat until smooth.

Scrape the batter into the prepared pan and bake for 40 to 45 minutes, or until the top is golden and a cake tester inserted in the center comes out clean. Set the cake pan on a wire rack to cool for 20 minutes. Then invert the cake onto the rack to cool completely. Wrap the cake in plastic wrap and chill in the freezer until slightly firm, about 15 minutes.

MEANWHILE, MAKE THE CUSTARD: In a small saucepan, bring the cream to a simmer. In a bowl, beat the whole egg, egg yolks, sugar, and cornstarch together until light and lemon-colored, about 3 minutes. Gradually whisk the hot cream into the egg mixture to warm it. Transfer the warmed egg mixture to the saucepan and cook over medium heat, stirring constantly, until thick, about 2 minutes. Remove from the heat and stir in the vanilla. Strain the custard through a fine sieve and set in a large bowl of ice water to quick-cool to room temperature. Cover and refrigerate until thoroughly chilled.

PREPARE THE GANACHE: Place the chocolate in a medium bowl. In a small saucepan, bring the cream and butter to a simmer. Stir in the sugar. Pour the hot cream mixture over the chocolate. Let stand, covered, for 5 minutes, then stir until smooth. Let cool to room temperature.

TO ASSEMBLE: With a long serrated knife, carefully slice the chilled cake horizontally into two layers. Place the bottom cake layer on a 9-inch cardboard round. Place the layer on a rack set over a cookie sheet. Spread the top of the cake with the chilled vanilla custard. Gently top with the second cake layer. Spread the ganache evenly over the sides and top of the cake. Chill in the refrigerator for 20 minutes to set.

# Chocolate Raspberry Rhapsody

Preheat the oven to 350°. Spray a 5-cup ring mold with nonstick cooking spray.

MAKE THE CHOCOLATE RING: In a food processor, combine the chocolate chips and sugar, then process until finely chopped. Add the boiling water and process until melted and smooth. Add the butter in three additions, processing briefly each time. Add the eggs, liqueur, vanilla, and salt. Process until well blended.

Pour the mixture into the prepared ring mold. Place the mold in a larger pan and fill the pan with 2 inches of boiling water. Bake for 1 hour, or until firm to the touch; a knife inserted in the center should come out clean.

Remove the mold from the water bath and let cool for 1 hour on a rack. Cover and refrigerate for at least 3 hours.

MAKE THE RASPBERRY CREAM: In a small bowl, beat the cream with the jam, sugar, and vanilla until soft peaks form.

TO ASSEMBLE: Run a knife around the edges of the mold and invert the ring onto a serving dish. Pipe a ring of raspberry cream rosettes around the base of the ring. Fill the center of the ring with the remaining raspberry cream. Garnish the ring with fresh raspberries.

### CHOCOLATE RING
*1 ¼ cups semisweet chocolate chips*
*1 cup sugar*
*½ cup boiling water*
*2 sticks (1 cup) unsalted butter, softened*
*4 large eggs*
*2 tablespoons raspberry liqueur*
*2 teaspoons vanilla extract*
*⅛ teaspoon salt*

### RASPBERRY CREAM
*1 cup heavy cream*
*2 tablespoons seedless red raspberry jam*
*2 tablespoons sugar*
*2 teaspoons vanilla extract*

*Fresh raspberries, for garnish*

YIELD: *16 servings*

# Rum-Soaked Chocolate Malibu

## RUM SYRUP
*½ cup sugar*
*½ cup minced pitted prunes*
*¼ cup water*
*¼ cup dark rum*
*2 teaspoons instant coffee granules*

## CAKE
*1¾ cups all-purpose flour*
*½ cup unsweetened cocoa powder*
*¾ teaspoon baking soda*
*¼ teaspoon baking powder*
*¼ teaspoon salt*
*1 stick (½ cup) unsalted butter*
*2 cups sugar*
*3 large eggs*
*2 teaspoons vanilla extract*
*2 ounces unsweetened chocolate, melted*
*1⅓ cups buttermilk, at room temperature*

## CHOCOLATE GANACHE
*16 ounces semisweet chocolate, finely chopped*
*2 cups heavy cream*
*2 tablespoons sugar*

**YIELD:** *16 to 20 servings*

**PREPARE THE RUM SYRUP:** In a small saucepan, combine the sugar, prunes, and water. Bring to a boil over medium heat, stirring constantly. Boil for 2 minutes. Remove from the heat and stir in the rum and coffee granules. Cover and set aside to steep.

**MAKE THE CAKE:** Preheat the oven to 350°. Line an 11-by-17-inch jelly-roll pan with foil extending beyond the sides. Butter and flour the foil.

In a medium bowl, whisk together the flour, cocoa, baking soda, baking powder, and salt. In a large bowl with an electric mixer, cream the butter and sugar. Beat in the eggs one at a time, beating well after each addition.

Reserving the rum syrup, strain out the prunes and stir them into the batter along with the vanilla and melted chocolate. In three additions, alternately add the flour mixture and the buttermilk, beating well after each addition.

Transfer the batter to the prepared pan and bake for 30 minutes, or until the center is set. Cool in the pan on a rack for 20 minutes. Then invert onto a rack, remove the foil, and cool to room temperature, about 1 hour.

**MEANWHILE, MAKE THE CHOCOLATE GANACHE:** Place the chocolate in a medium bowl. In a medium saucepan, bring the cream to a simmer. Add the sugar and stir to dissolve. Pour the hot cream over the chocolate. Let stand for 5 minutes, then stir until smooth. Quick-chill in the refrigerator for about 45 minutes, then let sit at room temperature to reach a spreadable consistency.

**TO ASSEMBLE:** Trimming off the outer edges, cut the cake crosswise into three 5-by-10-inch pieces. Cut out a piece of cardboard the same size and place a cake piece on the cardboard (this is the bottom layer). Prick the surface of all three pieces of cake with a toothpick. Brush the cake with the reserved rum syrup. Spread the bottom layer with ¾ cup of the chocolate ganache. Top with a second layer. Spread the second layer with another ¾ cup of chocolate ganache. Top with the last layer and frost the tops and sides with the remaining chocolate ganache. Chill in the refrigerator for 30 minutes to set.

# Triple-Layer Chocolate Peanut Butter Cheesecake

Butter and flour the bottom of a 9-inch springform pan. Butter (but do not flour) a second 9-inch springform pan that is 3 inches deep.

MAKE THE CRUST: In a food processor, process the Fudge Cookies and peanuts to fine crumbs. Add the butter and process just until the crumbs are moistened. Press the crust mixture into the bottom and halfway up the sides of the 3-inch-deep springform.

Preheat the oven to 300°. Place a roasting pan partially filled with water below the rack the cheesecake will bake on.

PREPARE THE CHOCOLATE LAYER: In a large bowl with an electric mixer, beat the cream cheese and sugar until smooth. Beat in the eggs one at a time, beating well after each addition. Beat in the sour cream and vanilla. Beat in the chocolate. Dividing the batter in half, pour into the prepared springform pans. Bake the cakes for 1 hour. Turn the oven off and leave the cheesecakes in the oven for 45 minutes. Cool in the pans on a rack for 30 minutes, then refrigerate until firm, about 4 hours. Remove the sides of the springforms.

MAKE THE PEANUT BUTTER LAYER: In a medium bowl, blend the peanut butter and butter until smooth. Beat in the confectioners' sugar and vanilla. Spread the peanut butter mixture over the chilled cheesecake with the crust. Remove the cheesecake from the bottom of the other springform and invert on top of the peanut butter layer.

PREPARE THE TOPPING: Place the chocolate in a small bowl. In a small saucepan, bring the cream to a simmer. Pour over the chocolate. Let stand, covered, for 5 minutes, then stir until smooth. Refrigerate the ganache until chilled but not firm. With an electric mixer, slowly beat the ganache until thickened and smooth; be careful not to overbeat or the ganache will break.

Spread the ganache on top of the cheesecake and halfway down the sides to meet the edge of the crust. Cover the ganache on the top and sides with the chopped peanuts.

## CRUST
*10 Fudge Cookies with White Chocolate (page 24)*
*1 cup unsalted peanuts*
*4 tablespoons unsalted butter, melted*

## CHOCOLATE LAYER
*1½ pounds cream cheese*
*1½ cups (packed) light brown sugar*
*4 large eggs*
*1 cup sour cream*
*1 tablespoon vanilla extract*
*16 ounces semisweet chocolate, melted*

## PEANUT BUTTER LAYER
*¾ cup creamy peanut butter*
*3 tablespoons unsalted butter*
*¾ cup confectioners' sugar*
*1 teaspoon vanilla extract*

## TOPPING
*6 ounces milk chocolate, chopped*
*1 cup heavy cream*
*1 cup finely chopped unsalted peanuts*

YIELD: *One 9-inch layered cheesecake*

# *Fudgy Studded Buttercream Cake*

### CAKE

*1¾ cups all-purpose flour*
*1¾ cups granulated sugar*
*1 teaspoon baking soda*
*2 sticks (1 cup) unsalted butter*
*2 cups plus 2 tablespoons water*
*2½ cups unsweetened cocoa powder*
*2 large eggs*
*1 tablespoon vanilla extract*
*½ cup buttermilk*

### CHOCOLATE GANACHE

*1 cup heavy cream*
*2 tablespoons granulated sugar*
*10 ounces semisweet chocolate, finely chopped*

### FUDGE FROSTING

*2 sticks (1 cup) unsalted butter*
*½ cup unsweetened cocoa powder*
*2 teaspoons vanilla extract*
*4 cups confectioners' sugar*
*¼ cup milk*

*¾ cup chopped walnuts, toasted*

YIELD: *One 9-inch layer cake*

Preheat the oven to 350°. Butter and flour two 9-inch cake pans.

MAKE THE CAKE: In a small bowl, whisk together the flour, granulated sugar, and baking soda.

In a heavy saucepan, combine the butter and water and cook until the butter is melted. Whisk in the cocoa and bring the mixture to a boil. Remove from the heat, transfer to a large bowl, and set aside to cool.

Add the eggs, one at a time, to the cocoa mixture, beating well after each addition. Beat in the vanilla. In two additions, alternately add the flour-sugar mixture and the buttermilk, beating well after each addition.

Pour the batter into the prepared pans and bake for 35 to 40 minutes, or until a cake tester inserted into the center comes out clean. Cool in the pans on a rack for 20 minutes. Then invert the cakes onto the racks to cool completely.

MEANWHILE, MAKE THE GANACHE: In a medium saucepan, bring the cream and granulated sugar to a boil. Remove from the heat and stir in the chocolate until melted. Refrigerate the ganache until firm enough to spread.

PREPARE THE FROSTING: In a medium bowl with an electric mixer, cream the butter. Beat in the cocoa and vanilla. In three additions, alternately beat in the confectioners' sugar and milk. If the frosting is too soft to spread, chill.

TO ASSEMBLE: Spread ¾ cup of ganache over the bottom layer. Top with the walnuts. Invert the top layer and spread ¾ cup of the fudge frosting on the *bottom*. Place the top layer, frosting-side down, on top of the bottom layer. Spread 1 cup of the frosting over the sides of the cake, and frost the top lightly with ½ cup. With a #21 star tip, pipe a ring of frosting rosettes around the outer rim of the cake. Then, with the same star tip, pipe a circle of ganache rosettes just inside the first ring. Continue alternating rings of frosting and ganache rosettes until the entire top of the cake is covered.

114

MAKE THE COOKIES: In a medium bowl, cream the butter and sugar. Beat in the eggs and vanilla. Blend in the flour. Chill the dough for 1 hour.

Preheat the oven to 325°. Roll the dough into 24 balls and place 2 inches apart onto ungreased cookie sheets. Flatten the cookies with the bottom of a glass and bake for 14 to 16 minutes, or until the edges turn golden. Transfer to racks to cool.

MEANWHILE, MAKE THE MOUSSE: Place the chocolate in a medium bowl. In a small heavy saucepan, bring ½ cup of the cream to a boil. Pour the hot cream over the chocolate and let stand, covered, for 5 minutes, then stir until smooth. Transfer the chocolate cream to a medium bowl.

In another medium bowl, beat the remaining ½ cup plus 2 tablespoons cream with the confectioners' sugar and vanilla until soft peaks form. Fold one-third of the whipped cream into the chocolate cream to lighten it. Gently but thoroughly fold in the remaining whipped cream. Refrigerate until firm.

MAKE THE CREME ANGLAISE: In a heavy medium saucepan, dissolve the granulated sugar in the water over low heat, stirring constantly. Increase the heat to medium-high and boil without stirring until the syrup turns a deep amber. Remove the pan from the heat and stir in the hot cream (be careful, it will bubble rapidly). Stir until smooth.

In a small bowl, whisk the egg yolks. Slowly beat in 1 cup of the hot caramel sauce to warm the egg yolks. Transfer the warmed egg yolks to the pan and cook over medium heat, stirring constantly, until the crème anglaise thickens and lightly coats the back of a spoon. Do not boil. Strain the sauce through a fine-mesh sieve and stir in the butter and vanilla. Keep warm.

TO ASSEMBLE: With a pastry bag fitted with a star tip, pipe rosettes of mousse over a cookie and top with a second cookie; decorate the top with cocoa powder dusted through a heart-shaped stencil. Spoon ¼ cup of the warm crème anglaise onto a small plate and place a floating heaven on top.

### BUTTER COOKIES
*1 stick (½ cup) unsalted butter*
*⅔ cup sugar*
*2 large eggs*
*1 teaspoon vanilla extract*
*1 cup plus 2 tablespoons all-purpose flour*

### DARK CHOCOLATE MOUSSE
*5 ounces semisweet chocolate, finely chopped*
*1 cup plus 2 tablespoons heavy cream*
*1 tablespoon confectioners' sugar*
*½ teaspoon vanilla extract*

### CARAMEL CREME ANGLAISE
*¾ cup granulated sugar*
*¼ cup water*
*2½ cups light cream, scalded*
*4 large egg yolks*
*1 stick (½ cup) unsalted butter, softened*
*2 teaspoons vanilla extract*

*Unsweetened cocoa powder, for garnish*

YIELD: *12 servings*

# Chocolate Torte with Raspberry Sauce

### TORTE
*2½ sticks (1¼ cups) unsalted butter*
*20 ounces semisweet chocolate, finely chopped*
*1 tablespoon vanilla extract or coffee liqueur*
*6 large eggs, at room temperature*

### GLAZE
*⅓ cup heavy cream*
*⅓ cup semisweet chocolate chips*

### RASPBERRY SAUCE
*Two 12-ounce packages unsweetened frozen raspberries*
*½ cup granulated sugar*
*2 tablespoons orange juice*

*Whipped cream, fresh raspberries, and Chocolate Leaves (page 102), for garnish*

**YIELD:** *One 8½-inch torte*

Preheat the oven to 400°. Butter the bottom and sides of an 8½-inch springform pan. Wrap the pan tightly in 2 layers of aluminum foil to keep the pan dry in the water bath. Place the springform in a large roasting pan and set aside.

**MAKE THE TORTE:** In a double boiler, melt the butter and chocolate. Stir until smooth. Remove from the heat and stir in the vanilla or coffee liqueur.

In a medium bowl, beat the eggs. Set the bowl over a pan of simmering water and whisk the eggs until they are warm, about 3 minutes. Remove from the heat and beat the eggs with an electric mixer at high speed until light and tripled in volume, 4 to 5 minutes.

Transfer the chocolate mixture to a large bowl and add one-fourth of the eggs. Mix thoroughly to lighten the chocolate. Gently fold the remaining eggs into the chocolate mixture. Transfer immediately to the prepared springform. Pour hot water into the roasting pan until it reaches halfway up the sides of the springform.

Bake for 18 minutes; the center will still be jiggly when removed from oven. Remove from the water bath and cool to room temperature, about 45 minutes. Remove the foil.

**MEANWHILE, MAKE THE GLAZE:** In a small saucepan, bring the cream to a simmer. Remove from the heat and add the chocolate chips. Cover for 15 minutes, then stir the mixture until smooth. Let cool to room temperature. Pour the glaze over the torte, then chill the torte in the refrigerator until firm, 6 to 8 hours.

**PREPARE THE SAUCE:** Drain the berries in a fine-mesh sieve set over a bowl; press gently on the berries to remove as much juice as possible. Transfer the juice to a small saucepan and reduce to about ⅓ cup. Return the reduced juice to the bowl and stir in the sugar and orange juice. With a wooden spoon, press the raspberries through the strainer into the bowl. Stir to combine the purée with the juice.

Run a knife around the edge of the torte to loosen it, then remove the sides of the springform pan. Serve the chilled torte with the raspberry sauce. Garnish with whipped cream, fresh raspberries, and Chocolate Leaves.

*After gently warming eggs over simmering water, beat them with an electric mixer until they are tripled in volume and cool to the touch.*

*Far left, pour hot water into the roasting pan to come halfway up the sides of the springform pan. Near left, before pouring on the glaze, use a knife to loosen the edges of the torte from the springform so that when the pan is removed later it will not stick to the glaze.*

# Triple Chocolate Suicide

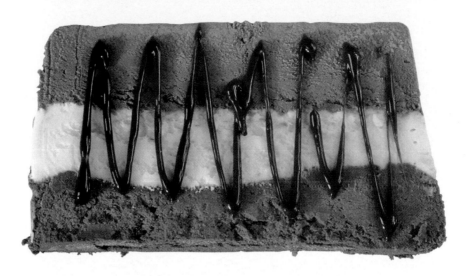

8 ounces white chocolate, finely
chopped
8 ounces milk chocolate, finely
chopped
6 ounces semisweet chocolate, finely
chopped
3 cups heavy cream
2 teaspoons instant coffee granules,
preferably espresso

Raspberry Sauce (page 116) or Super
Hot Fudge Sauce (page 79)

YIELD: 12 servings

Line a 6-cup terrine or loaf pan with foil so that the foil extends 2 inches beyond the two short ends.

Place the white chocolate, milk chocolate, and semisweet chocolate in 3 separate bowls.

In a medium saucepan, bring the cream to a simmer. Pour 1 cup of the warm cream over the white chocolate, 1 cup of the cream over the milk chocolate, and the remaining 1 cup cream over the semisweet chocolate. Stir each of the mixtures, while the cream is still warm, until melted and smooth.

Add the instant coffee to the milk chocolate mixture and, with an electric mixer, beat the mocha mixture until it is the consistency of sour cream, 4 to 5 minutes. Spread the mixture in the bottom of the prepared terrine. Freeze until just firm, about 30 minutes.

Beat the white chocolate mixture until the consistency of sour cream, 4 to 5 minutes. Spread over the mocha layer. Freeze until the white chocolate layer is just firm, about 30 minutes.

Meanwhile, beat the semisweet mixture until the consistency of sour cream, 4 to 5 minutes. Spoon this mixture over the white chocolate layer and smooth the top. Cover with foil and freeze until firm, 3 hours or overnight.

Lift up the foil to remove the terrine from the pan. Invert the terrine onto a platter and remove the foil. Cut the terrine into ½- to ¾-inch slices. Serve the terrine with Raspberry Sauce or Super Hot Fudge Sauce. (If using the Super Hot Fudge Sauce, cook the sauce for a shorter amount of time than called for in the recipe to produce a chocolate syrup rather than a thick fudge sauce.)

# Index

❖

## Acknowledgments

The author and editors would like to thank the following people for their assistance in the preparation of this volume:

**Glendale, California:** Carry Brentner. **Newtown, Connecticut:** Kathy Farrell-Kingsley. **Parsippany, New Jersey:** Ann Smith. **New York, New York:** Sara Abalan, Marie Baker-Lee, A. J. Battifarano, Amy Brummer, Catherine Ann Chatham, Georgia Downard, Elizabeth Fassberg, Rainer Fehringer, Cathy Garvey, Dave Mager, Sue Paige, Diane Simone Vezza, Andrea B. Swenson. **Park City, Utah:** Lavita Wai. **Alexandria, Virginia:** Leslie Beal Bloom, Peter Brett, Lisa Cherkasky, Marie F. Piraino, Ellen Robling, Barbara Sause, Tracey Seaman.

*Special thanks to* E. G. Perry and Michael Lunter. ***Extra-special thanks to*** Jessica, Jenessa, Jennifer, Ashley, and McKenzie Fields.